Railway backing. Included is the building of the California Southern north from San Diego, the coming of the Atchison, Topeka & Santa Fe, and the development of various smaller railroads like the California Pacific, Western Pacific, and others which formed California's railroad network.

Railroads, controlling not only the land but the politicians as well, set their own freight rates and ran California's government. This story is filled with California's growth and change over 61 exciting years. Described is how the reformers were victorious over the hated railroad monopoly. Brought to life once again are the many characters who built the railroad lines, and those who fought the carriers for reform.

California's Railroad Era 1850-1911 presents an outstanding and exotic picture of California's railroads. A brilliant text and captions complement the illustrations and maps, and take the reader back to the time when the railroads ruled the Golden State.

CALIFORNIA'S RAILROAD ERA
1850-1911

Ward McAfee

Golden West Books
San Marino, California

CALIFORNIA'S RAILROAD ERA 1850-1911
Copyright © 1973 by Ward McAfee
All Rights Reserved
Published by Golden West Books
San Marino, California 91108 U.S.A.

Library of Congress Catalog Card No. 73-18280
ISBN No. 87095-048-7

CIP

Library of Congress Cataloging in Publication Data

McAfee, Ward.
    California's railroad era, 1850-1911.

    Bibliography: p.
    1. Railroads--California--History.   I.   Title.
HE2771.C2M3   385'.09794   73-18280
ISBN 0-87095-048-7

Golden West Books
A Division of Pacific Railroad Publications, Inc.

P.O. BOX 8136 • SAN MARINO, CALIFORNIA • 91108

4

To Lois

Virgin timber towered above the tracks on Southern Pacific's Shasta Route, as passenger trains such as this worked their way between the San Francisco Bay region and Portland. — Guy L. Dunscomb Collection

Introduction

I N AN ERA when air transportation has replaced railroads as the most important means of passenger service, it is easy to forget the historic significance of California's railroad era. Much of the evidence supporting the validity of Frederick Jackson Turner's thesis regarding the importance of the frontier in American history is encompassed in the story of the first transcontinental lines. California's role in this epoch was unquestionably basic, and many of the issues and controversies which characterized the opening of the West were epitomized, sometimes in dramatic fashion, in the state.

In like manner, the railroad era brought to sharp focus the problems and benefits of America's age of unbridled industrial expansion. Too often, as the author points out, it is easy to assess blame for the problems, rather than appreciate the complex conditions which gave rise to them. Equally, the economic and social benefits of industrial expansion have often been ignored. This account attempts to take a look at the entire panorama, and depict the situation as it was. It describes the emerging of a new force in California with all of its positive and negative complications and resultant effects on social and political attitudes.

In this well-documented volume, the author has brought together the results of large masses of research and presents a balanced account of one of the most colorful and significant periods in the history of the American West.

GLENN S. DUMKE.

March 27, 1973

The name *California Limited* was only slightly less old and romantic in railroad legend than the name Santa Fe Railway itself. It was the pride of the Chi- cago-Los Angeles service in 1895 as it raced toward Los Angeles a few minutes out of San Bernardino. — SANTA FE RAILWAY COLLECTION

Table of Contents

Land speculation, railroads, and local boosterism were usually interconnected during California's railroad era. This illustration depicts land speculators arriving by special Santa Fe train at the Escondido depot in 1910. The auctioneer has already begun to sell land parcels. — DONALD DUKE COLLECTION

Preface

IN THE early days of California's railroad development, railroad companies structured their rate schedules to discriminate in favor of terminal towns, in order to encourage the long haul and thereby maximize profits. Because of this, huge commercial empires dominated by favorably placed cities suddenly became temporarily possible. Not every locality could win contests to become a terminus. Some would have to play "back country" to others. One consequence of this situation was a heightening of local rivalries and jealousies, which would become the central issues of California's railroad era. In fighting to become a terminus and in arguing over rates that railroad companies should be allowed to charge, communities usually operated individually, for these were concerns which by their very nature pitted town against town. Later, as California's rail network was extended and developed, the conditions that had accentuated inter-community conflicts passed. Slowly, localities became aware of the real and imagined injustices they suffered in common at the hands of railroad corporations operating in a disorganized economy. Gross discrimination between places by companies, a factor which served to maximize community rivalries, declined with the emergence of transcontinental competition, allowing a greater harmony of interests among California's localities. While these changes were regretted and vainly opposed by some cities, most of California's rival communities welcomed them and in the end all became more amenable to state-wide action and governmental regulation. But before this came about, local rivalries frequently interacted with the state's railroads in interesting and eventful ways.

I am indebted to many persons and organizations who assisted in the production of this book. Professor Don Fehrenbacher first suggested the general topic and provided encouragement and advice as the work progressed. The American Philosophical Society provided financial assistance for research. The library staff at California State College, San Bernardino, and those of Stanford University, Huntington, and Bancroft libraries were always cooperative and often helpful far in excess of duty. A term's leave from teaching duties, generously granted by California State College, San Bernardino, supplied the time necessary to complete the project. Lois and William McAfee, and William Attwater provided the editorial assistance without which this book would never have achieved whatever readability it possesses. Of course, I alone am responsible for any errors in the manuscript. Parts of several chapters have already appeared as articles in the *Pacific Historical Review*. "Local Interests and Railroad Regulation in California During the Granger Decade" appeared in February 1968, and "A Constitutional History of Railroad Rate Regulation in California, 1879-1911" followed in its August 1968, issue.

WARD McAFEE.

San Bernardino, California
September 1973

PART
ONE

Dreams and Plans

Women were scarce during California's gold rush, a fact that made the need for a transcontinental railroad all the more pressing. Nevertheless California's desires for safe overland transport had to wait a generation. — WELLS FARGO BANK HISTORY ROOM

1

Arguments for a
Transcontinental Railroad

URING THE 1850's, California's first decade of American rule, the new state's internal railroad development was minimal. Attention and practical planning in railroad affairs then focused on the dream of a Pacific railroad to connect East with West and bind the continent. Ironically, the intense desire of California's communities for the construction of this road would ultimately delay its progress by their bickering over the proper route of the line. But at the outset of California's railroad era, there was little awareness of this problem as the near-unanimous support of the various arguments for the Pacific railroad occupied the public mind. California's inhabitants dreamed of a transcontinental railroad as an end to their isolation. Like other mid-century Americans, they viewed the railroad as a means to promote cultural uniformity at home as a prelude to expanding their influence elsewhere. Likewise, a Pacific railroad would stabilize California's social and economic order, while increasing the wealth of state and nation. Irrespective of the interests of their particular communities, Californians agreed that the federal government owed their state the subsidization of the project, which would fulfill the promise of progress in a country and century supposedly dedicated to that ideal.

15

Vessels like the *S. S. Sonora*, of the Pacific Mail Steamship Company, provided the fastest transportoration to California in the 1850's. — WELLS FARGO BANK HISTORY ROOM

The loneliness of gold rush era men was an underlying source of California's dream of a transcontinental railroad. Many of the gold seekers viewed California only as a temporary residence, which would be left behind when their fortunes were made. Unhappily, few became rich, and many were left with nothing to show for their earlier hopes, marooned in California. They missed the warmth of life that they had left behind in "the states." Above all, they hungered for the feminine amenities, which were virtually unknown in their California. Hence, they demanded a transcontinental railroad, which could speedily carry them back home to their womenfolk or transport "those lovely girls" to a new home and certain marriage in California.[1]

Steamship travel, the fastest existing way to California, averaged a month from New York via the Isthmus of Panama to San Francisco. Letters, which were carried by the Pacific Mail Steamship Company, took even longer to arrive. On the other hand, a transcontinental railroad would deliver passengers from New York to San Francisco in an estimated week's time and speed postal communications with the East. Rumor held that the Pacific Mail Steamship Company paid Cornelius Vanderbilt $40,000 per month not to break its monopoly along the Pacific coast. A railroad would spell death to this "octopus" of the 1850's, whose high rates helped maintain the isolation of California.[2]

Travel from California to the East by steamship was hazardous, as well as slow and expensive. While arguing for a federally subsidized transcontinental railroad, California Congressman James A. McDougall angrily told his colleagues in the House that he could not visit his constituents without going into an atmosphere poisonous to his system. Not only was the journey by way of Panama unhealthy, but the routes overland were equally dangerous, for Indians could be as deadly as the dreaded cholera. What was needed was a modern mode of transportation overland, which could outrun the Indians and be far removed from the illnesses of the tropics. A transcontinental railroad would do this and deposit passengers in California in even better shape than travelers taking the relatively healthy but long clipper ship journey around the Horn.[3]

Speedy overland transport would also help stabilize California society and the business conditions in the West. A more responsible type of immigrant would supposedly come to California if the dangers of overland travel were lessened. "Merchants, traders, speculators, money dealers, lawyers, doctors, and others who consume without producing" tended to come by ocean transport, whereas "farmers, mechanics, and other producers" generally came by overland routes. The construction of the railroad would also bring more order to the marketing of goods by allowing the public's demand for items to be quickly met. Eastern merchandise coming to California by sea often arrived long after the initial demand had passed. The result of this situation was wild fluctation in the prices of commodities. Other commercial benefits would accompany the railroad. Insurance charges would certainly be less when importing by rail, and "sweating," an undesirable feature of freighting by ships, would be eliminated on a mechanical journey overland. The merchant would no longer receive "packages wet, discolored, and mouldy." And this would be greatly appreciated by the importer and his customers alike.[4]

Many different interests foresaw that their wealth would increase if the railroad were built. California's real estate owners predicted that immigration to the state would raise the prices of land. The cries from land speculators for a railroad grew most loud whenever passenger departures from California exceeded the monthly influx of strangers, such as following the social discord of the San Francisco Vigilance Committee of 1851. Increased foreign trade was also anticipated as a benefit from a transcontinental road. Market-conscious traders predicted that Asia with her millions would soon absorb much of the energy of western commerce. But which of the Occidental powers would come to dominate this trade? California's merchants regarded the British as their principal competitors. If John Bull seized the initiative by first constructing a canal across the Isthmus of Panama or a trans-Canadian railway, the commerce of the Orient would continue to be controlled by the enterprising British. "But give us a railroad," San Francisco's merchants pleaded, and the riches of China and Japan would pass through California on the way to the markets of Europe. Confidently, they predicted: "This Pacific railroad across our country will be the grave of British commercial supremacy."[5]

A federally financed transcontinental railroad was expected to save everyone money. Certainly the expanded trade with Asia over a Pacific railroad would fatten the public treasury with tariff income. And as people settled along the route, "immense tracts of land which now are useless to the General Government would be brought into market, and become of great value." Likewise, a railroad would improve the financial condition of the state. Better communications with the East would minimize the drain of gold from California to the "states." Governor John Bigler predicted that if a Pacific railroad were built, the families of miners would join their breadwinners in California, and the state's gold would be spent in the West.[6]

The iron horse would also allow a relatively inexpensive defense of the far western possessions of the United States while at the same time promoting national cultural unity. The internal threat of Mormonism would supposedly disintegrate upon the construction of a railroad across the Utah desert. Mormon wars, such as that experienced by the United States Army in 1857, would then become less likely, and the religion itself, some supporters of the railroad predicted, would wither and die, for it could "only con-

18

tinue to flourish in exclusiveness." Like the Mormon, hostile Indians could not hold out long after the construction of a transcontinental railroad, a result which would be most welcome in California, where Congressman McDougall claimed that state expenses for protecting her own frontier amounted to nearly a million dollars annually.[7]

America's mission to the rest of the world, as well as the extension of domestic uniformity, would be encouraged by the project. Construction of the railroad would facilitate trade and cultural interchange with the peoples of Asia and the Pacific islands, putting them "in contact with the arts of civilized life and the principles of Christianity, and thus hasten the amelioration and Christianization of the world." In fact, Pacific railroad boosters stated that it was the federal government's moral duty to build the road. During the 1850's, a trans-Atlantic cable was laid and the Czar of the Russias began building a railroad from St. Petersburg to Odessa, a distance of 1,600 miles. Certainly, they claimed, the federal government could match this progress.[8]

There was yet another reason why Californians thought that a federally subsidized railroad was warranted. Throughout the state, people felt that the federal government owed them something. Washington had collected millions of dollars in customs from western ports, and the drain of gold from California to the East certainly helped strengthen the national economy. But what in return had the government done for California? Nothing to improve the state's navigation and commerce and its very inefficient mail service. Despite claims by the eastern press that the Union gave more to California than it received from her, Californians were convinced that the federal government was discriminating against their state. And they believed that they knew the reasons for this unjust treatment. They were being blamed for the rise in sectional tensions that had resulted in the Compromise of 1850, by which California had become a state. But was it equitable for California to be made the scapegoat for the "fanaticism, headstrong obstinancy, and sectional prejudices" of the North and South? Westerners were united in giving a negative answer.[9]

Other states, such as Illinois, received generous federal subsidies for their railroad projects, but not California. An angry mood was rising in California because of this supposed bad treatment. "People cannot forever love that which spurns or neglects them," the *Alta California* noted as increasing threats were made to take California out of the Union. If the federal government sent an army to quell the movement to create a Pacific republic, Col. Thomas Jefferson Green predicted that it would fail. No army, he warned, could hold together near California's gold fields; "in such vicinity it would disappear like a lump of salt in a rain storm." A more famous California politico, Senator William Gwin, joined Green in warning that the Union could not be preserved unless the federal government took immediate action in supplying California's transportation needs.[10]

Californians made arguments and hurled threats, but nothing was done. Many of the arguments coming from the isolation of California were advocated by most Americans. Not only Californians would reap the benefits of a Pacific railroad. Expanded trade and religious influence in the Orient and South Pacific were desired by many easterners. The development of the West and resultant growth in national power and pride were widely held goals of the American people in general. Yet throughout the fifties, Congress remained deadlocked on the subject, failing to provide the aid needed for construction. What could explain this failure of democratic government to provide its citizenry with something so urgently and generally desired?

NOTES

1. *Daily Alta California,* April 24, 1854, 2:5; July 25, 1855, 2:3.
2. Memorial [*of the Citizens of San Francisco to the California State Legislature*] *Upon the Subject of Constructing a Railroad from the Pacific to the Valley of the Mississippi* (Sacramento, 1853), p. 10; *Report of the [California Senate] Committee on Federal Relations* (Sacramento, 1853), p. 4; *Report of the [California Senate] Committee on Commerce and Navigation* (Sacramento, 1858), pp. 3-4, 6, 11-12.
3. *Congressional Globe,* 33 Cong., 2 sess., p. 318; *Report of the [California Senate] Committee on Federal Relations* (Sacramento, 1853), p. 4; *Report of the [California Assembly] Committee on Federal Relations on the Pacific Railroad* (Sacramento, 1856), p. 6.
4. *Daily Alta California,* Aug. 28, 1852, 2:1; Oct. 24, 1853, 2:3; Dec. 26, 1854, 2:1.
5. *Ibid.,* Sept. 15, 1851, 2:1; April 11, 1852, 2:1; May 25, 1853, 2:1; Nov. 13, 1853, 2:4; June 17, 1854, 2:1; Jan. 22, 1857, 1:1.

6. *Report of the [California Assembly] Committee on Federal Relations on the Pacific Railroad. Submitted March 24, 1856* (Sacramento, 1856), p. 6; "Governor's Annual Message," *Journal of the California Assembly, Sixth Session* (Sacramento, 1855), pp. 45-46.

7. *Congressional Globe,* 33 Cong., 1 sess., p. 879; 33 Cong., 1 sess. (appendix), p. 864; *Annual Report of the [California] Surveyor General* (Sacramento, 1852), p. 20.

8. *Daily Alta California,* Sept. 4, 1853, 2:2; Oct. 28, 1853, 1:6; April 17, 1854, 1:7.

9. *Ibid.,* Mar. 2, 1851, 2:1; April 4, 1851, 2:1; Mar. 6, 1854, 2:1.

10. *Ibid.,* June 30, 1851, 2:1; Thomas Jefferson Green, *Letter to Hon. Robert J. Walker. Upon the Subject of Pacific Railroad, Sept. 19, 1853* (New York, 1853), p. 7; *Congressional Globe,* 33 Cong., 1 sess., p. 118.

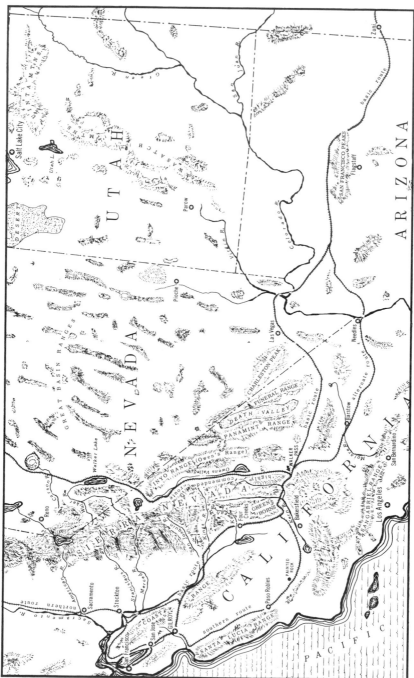

Many transcontinental rail routes were suggested in the 1850's. Joseph Walker advocated the above alternative routes before the California Senate's Committee on Public Lands in 1853.
COURTESY OF WALT WHEELOCK

2

A Question of Routes

ALTHOUGH Congress began seriously talking about a transcontinental railroad only after the acquisition of California in 1848, the idea was an old one, which some claimed dated back to the 18th century. Today, Asa Whitney is generally regarded as the prophet of the enterprise, for his advocacy of the project in 1846 helped revitalize an old dream. But whatever its sources, the idea remained without an influential champion until Senator Thomas Hart Benton pushed it as a primary issue before Congress in 1849. Encouraging Benton and other pro-railroad politicians were their constituents. Benton's own St. Louis held a mass meeting in 1849 to generate excitement on the subject. That year, Pacific railroad conventions also met in Memphis, New Orleans, and Boston, followed by one in Philadelphia in 1850. Each of these communities favored definite routes which would benefit its commerce, and every major city of the Mississippi Valley opposed any route which did not have it as the eastern terminus. Likewise, smaller communities foresaw themselves located along a favored route. Each city, town, and village of the United States was like Stone Landing of Mark Twain's *The Gilded Age* — "been waiting for a railroad more than four thousand years, and damme if she sha'n't have it [*sic*]."[1]

Urban railroad conventions thus not only encouraged discussion of a transcontinental railroad but also helped prevent any positive action on the subject. Largely agreeing on the need for a Pacific railroad, the representatives of America's communities could not agree where it should be built. Unfortunately, this disagreement could not easily be resolved, for mid-century America could afford to subsidize only one overland route. The great prize could not be shared by all. In addition to these community conflicts, sectional disagreements concerning the institution of slavery also helped prevent constructive dialogue on the subject in Congress. Northerners refused to consider a southern route, for that would aid in the expansion of the hated institution. Likewise, the South stood ready to veto any northern or central route which would aid in the growth of free states and the slow death of slavery, what southerners were already calling the "Southern decline." The South had to have the railroad, for as the *New Orleans Delta* declared: "This was the Aaron's rod that swallowed up all others. This was the great panacea, which is to release the South from its bondage to the North." Northerners, growing in population and political and economic power, saw the railroad as their due. There could be no compromise.[2]

Despite the divisiveness of local and sectional rivalries, national politicians submitted bills on the subject in the early fifties. In 1853, one such proposal to aid the construction of a moderately southern 35th parallel line was seriously considered but failed passage. The bill's author, California's Senator William Gwin, later saw that this was the closest that Congress came to aiding the project in the 1850's. Writing in his *Memoirs,* Gwin noted: "Mr. Fillmore, the President, was known to be in favor of the measure and would have signed the bill, and it would have become a law. This fact in history is the more important because it was very doubtful whether the newly elected President, Mr. Pierce, would approve such a bill." All doubt of Pierce's stand on the issue was obliterated in his state of the union message of 1854, in which he attacked the idea of the federal government subsidizing a Pacific railroad and all other "speculative schemes and extravagance." Noting the financial troubles of states during the panic of 1837, Pierce warned of the "danger of going too fast and too far." Aiding a railroad across the continent, he charged, would violate the Constitution of the United States, properly interpreted. Pacific railroad supporters would gloomily wait out Pierce's four-year term.[3]

Failing to pass Gwin's proposal in 1853, Congress settled upon a politic solution. Most congressmen were for aiding the Pacific railroad, but became deadlocked when discussing various routes. Accordingly, Gwin proposed that the Secretary of War order the Corps of Topographical Engineers to select scientifically the most practicable and economical railroad route to the Pacific coast. California's senator was not under the false illusion that science could substitute for politics in this matter. "If any route is reported to this body as the best," he told his colleagues, "those that may be rejected will always go against the one selected." He offered his suggestion, he concluded, "in the faint hope that some good may result." Mississippi's Jefferson Davis, who was then Secretary of War, made an elaborate report in 1855 to Congress upon the completion of the work. In 13 bulky tomes, congressmen read the results of the nine routes surveyed. The conclusions were in the interest of the extreme southern line, made practicable by the Gadsden Purchase of 1854. Northerners sneered that the Davis report proved what could be done by manipulating statistics. The fact that the 13 volumes were packed with much irrelevant information was used to discount the report's conclusions. Thus the efforts of the army engineers, far from resolving the question, succeeded only in sharpening local and sectional jealousies.[4]

While Congress remained deadlocked, the proponents of the various routes actively concentrated on shaping public opinion. Washington Territory's Governor Isaac Ingalls Stevens, the leading propagandist of the extreme northern route, felt that a road stretching from the northernmost cities of the Mississippi valley to Puget Sound would be superior, because it could be constructed with greater speed than any of the rival routes. On the western slope, workmen and equipment could be transported up the Columbia River ahead of tracklaying parties, while similar time-saving efforts could be made on the eastern side of the Rockies by making adequate use of the Missouri River. "Thus," he noted, "the route can be thrown into four divisions, on each of which the work can be commenced at both ends, so that eight sections may be worked at a time, affording extraordinary facilities to hasten the construction of the road." A road terminating at Puget Sound would also be closer to the anticipated trade boom with the Orient, the magnificent harbor of Puget Sound being not only "the nearest point on our whole Pacific coast to the ports of Asia" but also over 700 miles closer to the Mississippi River than San Francisco was. To those who charged that the heavy snows of winter would make his favored route impractical, Stevens answered that rails were being laid in the colder climates of Quebec and Russia. Besides, a northern Pacific railroad would be free from the blinding sand storms afflicting the southern route.[5]

For all of Stevens' arguments, the routes most seriously considered by the American public were in more southerly directions. Advocates of a central route pointed out that a central Pacific road would afford a compromise between the extremes of North and South, while at the same time providing "a medium between the bleakness of the north and the barrenness and sterility of the southern route." And where, asked Missouri's Benton, did the buffalo and other wild animals roam in their treks across the continent? The central route, being favored by beasts of instinct, was thus the "natural" route. Southerners were quick to retort that level land rather than forage for animals should be the primary consideration in the selection of the right of way. A southern route would skirt both the snow and high peaks of its rivals. "What great advantage," asked Louisiana's Senator Solomon W. Downs, "would there be in having a railroad in a route where it could be kept open only half the year?"[6] This charge against the central Pacific route was the best weapon in the arsenal of southern arguments; so much so in fact that John Charles Frémont, the son-in-law of Senator Benton, crossed the Rockies and Sierra during the winter of 1853-1854 in an effort to prove the southerners wrong. Arriving in San Francisco on April 16, 1854, Frémont denied rumors that starvation and cold had taken seven of his party. The winter had been unusually severe, claimed the pathfinder, admitting only to the death of one man. Having made his point, he hurried east to "lay before the public the results" of his exploration.[7]

Southerners also minimized the drawbacks of their favored routes. The danger of the Apaches, claimed the *San Diego Herald*, was greatly overrated: "The main object in making attacks, like that of all other Indian tribes, is to steal stock, and if a proper guard is kept, and they find that to obtain animals they are obliged to fight, they will give no trouble." And if they did, a southern Pacific railroad would aid in their elimination. Likewise, the existence of a main artery of American military power along the southern border would serve the expansion of the United States into the northern Mexican states. Another charge was that the southern route was too dry to support the needs of a railroad and the settlers it would bring. Along the 32nd parallel route, wrote the *San Diego Herald*, "there is no stretch of over twenty-eight miles without water." A southern railroad could also be constructed for less money than any of its rivals. Flat land and dry weather would cut costs and huge land grants by the state of Texas would help in reducing the aid of the federal government needed for the project.[8]

Such were the arguments given in favor of the respective routes before Congress. But to the growing frustration of Californians, no action was taken. Some reasoned that the deadlock could be broken if the far West had more power in Congress, and so the first movement to divide California into several states was born. The attempt was also supported by men of southern sympathies, desirous of expanding slavery, and by southern California rancheros, anxious to preserve their land holdings from existing state tax policies that favored northern California. Ultimately the movement failed, after coming close to succeeding at the end of the decade.[9] In the mid-fifties, Californians blamed forces outside the West for the lack of a transcontinental railroad. The obstructionism of President Pierce, local and sectional jealousies that existed in the eastern states, and California's small amount of political influence in Washington, D.C., were pointed to as the causes of failure. However, by the end of the decade, western supporters of the railroad would come to realize that local jealousies and rivalries spawned along the Pacific slope also contributed to the congressional deadlock denying their dream.

NOTES

1. Joseph Ellison, *California and the Nation, 1850-1869: A Study of the Relations of a Frontier Community With the Federal Government* (Berkeley, 1927), p.

141; *New York Tribune,* May 8, 1869 (found in Bancroft Scraps [Bancroft Library, University of California, Berkeley], LXXX, 1173-1176); Hubert Howe Bancroft, *History of California* (San Francisco, 1886), IV, 222-225, VII, 508-510; Theodore H. Hittell, *History of California* (San Francisco, 1897), IV, 447; Mark Twain and Charles Dudley Warner, *The Gilded Age, A Tale of Today* (New York, 1873), I, 159.

2. Robert R. Russel, "The Pacific Railway Issue in Politics Prior to the Civil War," *Mississippi Valley Historical Review,* XII (1925), 192.

3. William H. Ellison, ed., "Memoirs of Hon. William M. Gwin," *California Historical Society Quarterly,* XIX (1940), 174-175; *Daily Alta California,* Jan. 1, 1855, 2:6.

4. *Congressional Globe,* 32 Cong., 2 sess., pp. 798-799; *New York Tribune,* May 8, 1869 (Bancroft Scraps, LXXX, 1173-1176); *New York Herald,* May 10, 1869 (Bancroft Scraps, LXXX, 1180-1182); *Daily Alta California,* June 11, 1854, 1:7.

5. Isaac I. Stevens, *Letter of Isaac I. Stevens, Delegate from Washington Territory, to the Railroad Convention of Washington and Oregon, Called to Meet at Vancouver, W.T., May 20, 1860* (Washington City, 1860), pp. 7-18.

6. *Congressional Globe,* 31 Cong., 2 sess., p. 132; *ibid.,* 32 Cong., 2 sess., p. 340; *Daily Alta California,* Aug. 7, 1854, 2:1.

7. *Daily Alta California,* Mar. 10, 1854, 2:3; April 17, 1854, 2:2; April 21, 1854, 2:1; April 24, 1854, 2:1,3.

8. Lewis B. Lesley, "The Struggle of San Diego for a Southern Transcontinental Railroad Connection, 1854-1891" (Ph.D. dissertation, University of California, Berkeley, 1933), p. 103; *San Diego Herald* quoted in *Daily Alta California,* Jan. 7, 1858, 1:4; Russel, "The Pacific Railway Issue in Politics," p. 190.

9. Throughout most of the 1850's, California was the only state from the Pacific coast; and because of the famous Gwin-Broderick feud, California was represented by only one senator from 1855 to 1857. *Daily Alta California,* Feb. 16, 1855, 2:3; April 19, 1855, 2:1.

3

Local Rivalries and Transportation Needs

CALIFORNIA and the West have long been regarded as principal sources of "rugged individualism" and the American competitive spirit. There is, perhaps, some truth in this popular belief. Less widely appreciated is the evidence that these traits were often manifested in the form of communities operating as units. Daniel Boorstin has written that

> in the upstart cities of the West the characteristic and most fertile competition was a competition among communities. We have been misled by slogans of individualism. . . . Where individual and community prosperity were so intermingled, competition among individuals was also a competition among communities.

Local rivalries were not confined just to the larger cities, for Californians were capable of raising dreams of commercial greatness out of little more than fertile imaginations. In their eyes a log house could appear a "compactly built town, with all creation as its suburbs." The editor of a newspaper at Oroville, a small town on the Feather River, could predict that someday his community would receive the transcontinental railroad. Small villages like San Diego could boldly claim victory over powerful San Francisco for the prize of terminus of the Pacific railroad. In an age of unbounded optimism such talk was often taken seriously.[1]

Characteristically, San Franciscans tried to reassure themselves that San Diego and other competitors posed no threat. "Nature has marked this city as the emporium of the Pacific," their newspapers proclaimed. "San Francisco must be to the Pacific, and to the Union, what Venice was to the Mediterranean and Italy — what London is to the Atlantic and Great Britain." Yet San Francisco was not so confident as to ignore rival communities. And so, in late 1853, the bay city held a railroad convention in hopes of gaining state-wide support for her railroad aspirations. Unhappily, the delegates engaged in "differences of opinion of a local character." Surprised at the independence of their guests, the hosts periodically hissed down those who made proposals not in the commercial interests of San Francisco. Ending inconclusively, the convention was, in the words of the *Alta California,* a "miserable abortion." Benicia and Vallejo, communities along the Carquinez Straits and especially active in the late convention, had long stood out in making unneighborly threats to San Francisco's hopes. Placed at the northern tip of a long peninsula, San Francisco was poorly situated to be the western terminus. Why not start the railroad at Benicia or Vallejo, both deep water ports, rather than make the detours necessary to get to San Francisco? Such suggestions brought down an avalanche of insults by bay city commercial reporters, who predicted that Benicia would burst itself "in vainly attempting, like the frog in the fable to swell its size to the dimensions of an ox."[2]

Realistically, San Francisco understood that abortive conventions and abusive language would not insure its commercial prominence. Constructing railroads would. A railroad projected to be built to San Jose, under the name of the Pacific and Atlantic Railroad Company, had been organized in 1851. When completed down the peninsula, this line would serve as the first link of the transcontinental railroad and would insure San Francisco as the western terminus. But this dream was shattered by the financial panic of early 1855, ruining many of the capitalists sponsoring the project. I. C. Woods, President of the Pacific and Atlantic and a partner in one of the banking houses hardest hit by the financial storm, escaped his angry creditors by departing secretly for Australia. While economic gloom temporarily put expensive railroad projects to sleep, California's commercial men now felt the need for improved transcontinental transportation as never before. In their eyes, massive immigration to California from the East was the one escape from the state's economic depression. One or several wagon roads could be cheaply constructed across the plains to encourage the westward movement. With Congress embroiled in sectional disputes, Californians first looked to their legislature for assistance. For the next several years, California's local rivalries would primarily be exhibited in wagon road, not railroad, affairs.[3]

Early in 1855, an "Emigrant Road Committee" met at San Francisco's Musical Hall and passed a series of resolutions requesting state aid for a wagon road through the treacherous Sierra. To some degree, this committee provided the center of activity on the subject. But also, for years, several surveyor generals had been working quietly behind the scenes to cultivate grass roots support for staking the best route through the largely uncharted mountains. In their annual reports they had stressed the need for such activity and had subtly encouraged local interests by requesting information on possible routes from county surveyors. Predictably, each of the county surveyors from the Sierra region claimed the best route. Although every local promoter sang a different tune, the dissonance helped prod the legislature to action.[4] In late April 1855, "An Act to Provide for the Survey and Construction of a Wagon Road over the Sierra Nevada Mountains" was passed into law. One hundred thousand dollars was pledged to the building of one road, the western terminus of which would be Sacramento. The actual route taken to the eastern boundary of the state would be chosen by a special commission, after appropriate groundwork under the direction of the surveyor general. But to the rue of the latter, only $5,000 was appropriated for the necessary surveys. Ultimately, not-so-subtle appeals to local ambitions produced the aid. Surveyor General S. H. Marlette's appeal to the people of Camptonville exemplified this tactic:

> In Georgetown, Diamond Springs and Mud Springs, money has already been raised, and I have reason to believe that in Sonora, funds are now being raised to enable me to accomplish one important object of the Act. What will the citizens of Camptonville do? They have now a splendid opportunity to back the high opinion they entertain of their route.[5]

Unhappily for Camptonville and numerous other small communities, the route eventually selected was by way of Placerville in El Dorado county. Bids were then called for to construct the road, the low bid going to an L. B. Leach of Stockton. When authorities later discovered that Leach did not exist, suspicions rose that Stocktonians, interested in seeing the wagon road go over the Big Tree route some 40 miles south of Placerville, had conspired to obstruct the progress of the enterprise. Shortly afterwards, legal proceedings to contest the constitutionality of the act of 1855 were instituted, which resulted in the state supreme court voiding the measure in December 1856. The court's opinion stated that the proper procedures for passing such an act, as described in the state constitution, had not been followed. As Surveyor General Marlette had shown, local jealousies could be used to promote improvements in public transportation. However, they could also destroy such efforts. San Francisco's press accusingly looked to Stockton as the agent of obstruction. On the day of the supreme court's decision, the *Alta California* editorialized:

> The jealousy exhibited and continual war carried on between the people of the several counties who are favorable to one or another of the several routes have done more towards retarding the commencement and prosecution of the road than all other causes combined. The suicidal policy which they have pursued has proved seriously injurious to the best interests of the State, and prevented the carrying out of an enterprise second to none in importance ever projected in California.

The editorial failed to note that powerful steamship concerns, centered in San Francisco, were also suspected of killing this first concrete effort for better overland communications.[6]

Early in 1856, while the state-aided project expired, California's pleas for aid shifted to Congress. A petition of 75,000 signatures was raised by San Francisco's Emigrant Road Committee, under the new leadership of Captain William Tecumseh Sherman, and sent to Washington. Calling for a wagon road to be built over a central route, the petition was presented in two large folio volumes. Surprisingly, Congress responded favorably within a year's time. Although deadlocked by sectional hatreds and local jealousies on the Pacific railroad, Congress could compromise on the lesser prize of a wagon road. The reason for this was clear. The country could afford to build only one transcontinental railroad, but the Wagon Road Act of 1857 called for the construction of three roads, one major road over a north-central route terminating near Honey Lake, California, and two lesser ones through the southwest.[7]

Like all transportation measures, the Wagon Road Act evoked varying responses throughout California. People living in the San Joaquin and lower Sacramento valleys were most dissatisfied, for none of the western termini stipulated in the bill was easily accessible. However, Marysville and the northern part of the Sacramento valley were quite pleased with the work of Congress, which placed the main western terminus close by at Honey Lake. Eager to capitalize on her newly won advantage, Marysville held a convention in early April with the object of promoting a wagon road to Honey Lake. And by autumn, there was talk of a connecting railroad from Marysville to the tidewater at Benicia. The entire northern part of the state was aware of the opportunities and local rivalries created by the act, as manifested in a *Shasta Republican* editorial:

> Notwithstanding the many advantages possessed by Noble's Pass [Honey Lake route], those interested in more southern routes will make strenuous exertions to overcome them. Sacramento city will, if possible, induce the immigration to come by way of Carson Valley, and thence by the most practicable route to that city. In the San Joaquin Valley exertions will be made to bring immigration in by the Big Tree road. It is certain . . . that runners and handbills will be sent in abundance to the Humboldt River, for the purpose of slandering the Honey Lake road, and magnifying the advantages of other roads. Similar practices have been adopted in previous years, and it behooves us to do something to counteract their influence.[8]

As the largest town in the San Joaquin valley, Stockton had to overcome the disadvantages of location to tap the influx of coming seasons. Stockton's Big Tree route over the Sierra was already fairly well developed. In fact, in 1856-1857 most of the immigration to the state came by this highway. Nevertheless, Stocktonians were not satisfied with the achievements of the past and knew that only strenuous efforts to improve the Big Tree route could insure their city's position once the federal government's wagon roads

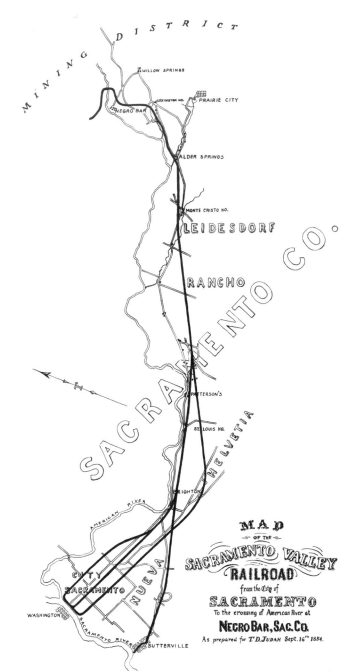

Map of the Sacramento Valley Railroad as prepared by T. D. Judah, September 16, 1854. — SOUTHERN PACIFIC COLLECTION

were developed. Not to be outdone, Stocktonians and delegates from surrounding counties met in convention at Mokelumne Hill, east of Stockton, to consider ways to meet the challenge. But nothing was done there to advance the interests of Stockton ahead of her rivals.[9]

Perhaps the most energetic community at this time was Sacramento. The city had become the stagecoach travel center of the state even before becoming its political capital. The Sacramento Valley Railroad Company, the first successful commercial railroad in the state, was completed from Sacramento to Folsom in February 1856, with one of the first locomotives on the line appropriately named *Sacramento*. The first transcontinental railroad also would be built eastward from Sacramento, but unable to foresee

The locomotive *Sacramento* of the Sacramento Valley Road, inaugurated an era of Sacramento's rail supremacy.

their city's future victories, Sacramentans in 1857 strenuously competed with their rivals for the best wagon road across the mountains. In early May, a wagon road convention was held composed mainly of delegates from Sacramento and Placerville, who vowed at that time to construct the road surveyed by the state in 1855 at their own expense. Aggressively fulfilling their objectives, the backers of the Sacramento-Placerville route kept several steps ahead of their competition. In 1858, a Placerville-based firm began constructing the western end of a transcontinental telegraph line among predictions that the Pacific railroad eventually would be built beside the wires. John Kirk, a federal government contractor of the Honey Lake route, had property investments in Placerville and spent many days surveying and improving the road leading there, although unauthorized to do so, thus facilitating traffic between Placerville and the principal federal wagon road. Finally, the propagandists of the Placerville route so outdid their competitors that the *Alta California* sarcastically observed: "We shall next hear that the best way to Heaven is through Placerville."[10]

While many local jealousies were enhanced by the passage of the Wagon Road Act, the enactment of another federal act in 1857, providing for the rapid delivery of mail overland, further accentuated local jealousies and fears. For years Californians, especially those in the southern part of the state and the interior valleys, had complained of the slow sea-going mail service. By the Overland Mail Act, they were to be relieved from this situation, as soon as Postmaster General Aaron Brown could choose a suitable contractor to carry the mail. Ignoring the law's provision that the bidding parties would select the route to be followed, Brown himself chose the route, with one eastern terminus at his home town of Memphis. In short, Butterfield and Company, the contractor picked by Brown to make a semi-weekly run to California, was to follow a path favored by the advocates of a southern Pacific railroad. This was significant in that settlements would certainly crop up along the route. Once this condition had materialized, a Pacific railroad would most probably follow.[11]

Inhabitants of the Honey Lake area, chief beneficiaries of congressional wagon road legislation, bemoaned the failure of the Postmaster General to cross their community with an overland mail route. Similarly, Sacramentans were infuriated with Brown's ox bow or horse shoe route, named for its indirect, semi-circle path from the Mississippi River to San Francisco. Northern Californians in general scorned the "chivalry instincts" of the Buchanan administration and especially damned the southern cabinet member whose instincts were wedded to the town of Memphis. But southern California only had praise for the Postmaster General's "foresight." In reality, northern California was not without a federally subsidized central overland mail route. Once a week, mail was delivered to California over the Placerville road, with the carrying company of Hockaday and Chorpenning receiving a subsidy of $320,000 annually. A monthly mail also came by way of a south-central path to Stockton for $79,999. But these were crumbs when compared to the feast of $600,000 per annum paid to Butterfield and Company for its semi-weekly service. It certainly appeared that the Buchanan administration was grooming the southern route for the Pacific railroad.[12]

Fears mounted in San Francisco when President Buchanan publicly came out in favor of a southern railroad route across the continent early in 1858. Would San Diego be *the* commercial metropolis of the Pacific slope in the future? The *Alta California* papered over the growing anxiety of the bay city with expressions of false confidence:

> One thing is certain — that whatever route may be adopted, San Francisco must be the western terminus, and nothing short of an absolute destruction of her great commercial position and advantages by a convulsion of nature, can rule it otherwise, President and Senators to the contrary notwithstanding.

With the settlement of the Kansas controversy and the resultant easing of sectional tensions in the spring of 1858, together with the return of prosperity to California, new life was given to the long-deferred subject of a transcontinental railroad. However, this rebirth was greeted with mixed feelings in San Francisco. Rival coastal communities were improving their competitive positions for the western terminus. San Diego possessed an ally in the White House, and the Puget Sound region was the beneficiary of a new western gold rush along the Fraser River. San Francisco's commercial greatness had been made by the first gold rush of 1848-1849, and knowledge of this history made bay-city residents genuinely fearful of the new northern rival.[13] However, proponents of the central route possessed sufficient ingenuity to meet these new challenges. In April 1859, both houses in Sacramento passed a joint resolution calling for a Pacific railroad convention to meet in San Francisco the following September. Because of the basis of representation described in the bill, northern California's delegates would be able to outvote both those sent from the southern part of the state and the Pacific northwest's representatives.[14]

San Francisco's commercial interests had been instrumental in bringing delegates from the Pacific coast together, and, maintain-

Col. J. B. Crockett

Local aspirations, in mid-19th century America, depended heavily upon the individuals who came forward to champion an urban or regional cause. The men represented here were most active on behalf of California. Col. J. B. Crockett, shown at the left, directed San Francisco's delegates in the Pacific Railroad Convention of 1859. Both Gwin and McDougall, representing California in Congress during the 1850's, made known to the nation their state's desire for a transcontinental railroad, but with little success. — BANCROFT LIBRARY

William Gwin

James A. McDougall

ing the initiative, bay-city delegates were first to make major proposals to the convention. Col. J. B. Crockett moved that San Francisco be promoted by the convention as the proper terminus of the Pacific railroad. Reaction was swift. "We have not come down from Oregon to select a terminus," shouted T. J. Dryer. "We might as well introduce a resolution fixing the terminus at Walla Walla, Puget Sound or any other important point in Oregon and Washington Territory." Concluding his speech, the delegate from Oregon warned that passage of Crockett's resolution "would cool the ardor of the members of the convention," an opinion shared by southern California's representatives. Seeing opportunity in dissention, Sacramento's L. A. Booth moved to amend the Crockett proposal to make "some point upon the Bay of San Francisco," rather than the city itself, the western terminus. The effort was transparent. If San Francisco became the terminus, the transcontinental railroad would have to dip 50 miles south before turning east toward the mountains. Such was the geography of the peninsula. But if "some point upon the Bay of San Francisco" were made the terminus, then Oakland, Vallejo, or Benicia might be chosen, which would make it more likely that track would be built eastward through Booth's Sacramento. Others were not so subtle. For example, delegate J. B. Frisbie of Solano "indulged in a regular and systematic denunciation of San Francisco," while describing the superior advantages of Benicia, the pride of his county. Despite such efforts, Crockett's resolution passed on the first day of the convention. However, the delegates from the Pacific northwest excused themselves from voting, explaining that "it was no matter to them what was done in California."[15]

The convention that had met to express the unity of western feeling upon the Pacific railroad was deeply divided. Yet only the decisions of the convention, and not a transcript of the heated debates, would be read in the eastern press. There would be at least a facade of unity presented by the Pacific coast. With this in mind, the *Alta California* noted:

> Up to this period a dozen different points along the coast of California, Oregon and Washington Territory, have had their advocates, and public sentiment upon this one branch of the Railroad question has been almost as much divided as it is upon

a like subject in the Atlantic States. The action of the convention tends to settle this dispute, and places the people of the Pacific coast as a unit before Congress and the nation.

However, convention leaders realized that the real disunity of the first session might result in a noisy, publicized rupture if concessions were not made. Early the next day, Col. Crockett made his move by offering three propositions:

1. That in the opinion of the Convention, there should be two western termini to the Pacific Railroad, to wit: one at the City of San Francisco, in the State of California; and the other on the waters of the Columbia river, or at Puget Sound.

2. That the Road should be immediately commenced from each of said termini — from the one by the people of California, and from the other by the people of Oregon and Washington Territory; with a view to unite them, if practicable, at some convenient point.

3. That the Legislatures of the States of California and Oregon be memorialized to establish in each an Internal Improvement Fund, to be devoted primarily to the prosecution of the work within the States respectively.[16]

These resolutions, which passed, allowed the delegates from California to use the convention for their local interests without precipitating an open rebellion by Oregon's Dryer and his northern colleagues.

The Californians then turned to selecting part of the route eastward from the San Francisco terminus. Crockett proposed a route from San Francisco to Stockton, by way of San Jose. Conceding the intensity of local feeling, he questioned the wisdom of deciding upon the route east of Stockton, from which the road could veer north or south or continue due east across the mountains. The decision of plotting the path of the locomotive to the eastern boundary of the state would be left to the legislature in Sacramento, and the clash of much local rivalry would be postponed. Also, by extending the line to Stockton, rather than stopping at San Jose, localism would be diminished, for if the route were drawn only south to San Jose the inference might be made that the convention was backing the idea of a southern route. Crockett had expressed a futile hope, for his route proposal heightened rather than tempered local jealousies in the convention. W. H. Rhodes, delegate from Butte county in northern California, was first to react. Recalling that the convention had already selected two western termini, Rhodes suggested that the entire routes from both termini to a point of junction should be selected. The state legislature, he observed, had called the convention into being to make such important decisions, yet Crockett was suggesting to shuttle the controversy back into the hands of the legislature. The motivation behind Rhodes' oratory was clear to his fellow delegates. With Oregon and Washington represented in the San Francisco convention, chances were good that a route selected there would traverse Butte county. But if the task were left to the state legislature, a more central route across the mountains would probably be chosen.[17]

Crockett's proposal was subtly designed to foster a central route over the Sierra. But some delegates, angered by Rhodes, pushed openly for the central route. Seeing danger in such a display, Col. Crockett pleaded with the convention to accept his suggestion. Little was known of the potential railroad routes across the mountains, he argued, and therefore the selection of the route beyond Stockton should be made by the legislature, after the proper scientific surveys. Shortly after his speech, the Crockett resolution passed by a vote of 38 to 18, with some delegates from the Pacific northwest joining the minority, and others not voting. Southern California's representatives also opposed this proposal.

Sectional hostility was high on the convention's last day. Another Oregon delegate, Thomas H. Pearne, complained of leaving "the whole question of direction of the road eastward from Stockton to the California legislature, which might extend it to the extreme southern route with which neither Oregon nor Washington Territory could connect." The action taken by the convention made him and his colleagues feel as if their presence had been skillfully used against the interests of their constituents. The delegates from southern California offered a more radical protest by walking out of the convention. With the facade of unity thus torn away, the majority in a final act declared in favor of the central route.[18] Theodore D. Judah, long active on the subject of the Pacific railroad and a delegate from Sacramento, was chosen to take the controversial resolutions to Congress. But the activities of the Pacific Railroad Convention would not prod Congress to action, for as the convention adjourned, abolitionist John Brown waited for violence in the hill country of western Virginia. His famous raid on Harper's Ferry in mid-October would help make congressional decision on the transcontinental railroad impossible until the catharsis of civil war.

NOTES

1. Daniel Boorstin, *The Americans, The National Experience* (New York, 1965), pp. 122-123; Mark Twain and Charles Dudley Warner, *The Gilded Age, A Tale of Today* (New York, 1873), I, 164; *Daily Alta California,* June 11, 1857, 1:1; July 15, 1853, 2:4; Aug. 21, 1854, 2:3.
2. *Daily Alta California,* May 25, 1853, 2:1; Oct. 4, 1853, 2:2; Oct. 5, 1853, 2:3-4; Dec. 14, 1854, 2:2; July 18, 1854, 2:1; Dec. 8, 1856, 1:4; Mar. 2, 1857, 2:4.
3. *Ibid.,* June 23, 1855, 2:1; Aug. 13, 1855, 1:3; April 12, 1856, 2:1; Hubert Howe Bancroft, *History of California,* VII, 536.
4. *Annual Report of the Surveyor General, Dec. 15, 1852* (Sacramento, 1853), p. 19; *Annual Report of the Surveyor General, Dec. 15, 1854* (Sacramento, 1855),p p. 6-7, 31, 40, 44, 51-52, 59, 90, 92-93.
5. *Annual Report of the Surveyor General, of the State of California* (Sacramento, 1856), pp. 12-13.
6. Chester L. White, "Surmounting the Sierras, The Campaign for a Wagon Road," *California Historical Society Quarterly,* VII (1928), 10; *The People ex rel. the Attorney General v. J. Neely Johnson et al.,* 6 Calif. Reports 499; *Daily Alta California,* Dec. 8, 1856, 2:2. For a contemporary account agreeing with the *Alta's* appraisal see Theodore Judah, *A Practical Plan for Building the Pacific Railroad* (Washington, D.C., 1857), p. 5.
7. *Congressional Globe,* 34 Cong., 3 sess. (appendix), p. 401; *Daily Alta California,* Mar. 27, 1856, 2:3; June 17, 1856, 2:2.
8. *Daily Alta California,* Mar. 31, 1857, 2:1; April 12, 1857, 2:1; Oct. 21, 1857, 1:2; April 16, 1857, 1:1 (*Shasta Republican* quoted).
9. White, *loc. cit.,* p. 13; *Daily Alta California,* April 11, 1857, 1:1; Mar. 25, 1857, 2:2.
10. Oscar O. Winther, *Express and Stagecoach Days in California* (Stanford, 1936), 87-88; Bancroft, *History of California,* VII, 538-539; Carl I. Wheat, "A Sketch of the Life of Theodore D. Judah," *California Historical Society Quarterly,* IV (1925), 223; W. Turrentine Jackson, *Wagon Roads West, A Study of Federal Road Surveys and Construction in the Trans-Mississippi West, 1846-1869* (Berkeley, 1952), pp. 203-205; *Daily Alta California,* May 14, 1857, 1:1; Oct. 7, 1858, 2:1; July 7, 1858, 1:6.
11. *Report of the [California Senate] Committee on Commerce and Navigation* (Sacramento, 1858), p. 4; Winther, *Express and Stagecoach Days,* pp. 161-164; LeRoy Hafen, *The Overland Mail, 1849-1869* (Cleveland, 1926), pp. 88-90.
12. *Daily Alta California,* Feb. 6, 1858, 1:2, Oct. 22, 1858, 1:6; Oct. 23, 1858, 1:1; Oct. 29, 1858, 1:7; Nov. 19, 1858, 1:4; Hafen, *Overland Mail,* pp. 115-116, 121.
13. *Daily Alta California,* Mar. 5, 1858, 2:1; Mar. 9, 1858, 2:1; April 7, 1858, 2:1; April 19, 1858, 1:3-4; June 12, 1858, 1:7-8.

14. William C. Fankhauser, *A Financial History of California, Public Revenues, Debts, and Expenditures* (Berkeley, 1913), p. 207; *Daily Alta California,* Aug. 15, 1859, 1:1; Sept. 21, 1859, 1:6.
15. *Daily Alta California,* Sept. 22, 1859, 1:4-7.
16. *Ibid.,* Sept. 22, 1859, 2:2; Sept. 23, 1859, 1:3-7.
17. *Ibid.,* Sept. 23, 1859, 1:3-7.
18. *Ibid.,* Sept. 25, 1859, 1:3-7.

TWO

The First
Transcontinental Railroad

The Sacramento Valley Railroad Company was the first corporate champion of Sacramento's dream to become the commercial center of California. The company's depot, shown above, was located on Front Street along the levee. — SOUTHERN PACIFIC COL-

4

Sacramento's Victory

SHORTLY after the Pacific Railroad Convention adjourned, news of a tremendous silver strike in Washoe, Nevada, filtered down the mountains. A new rush was on. Concentrated within a 30-mile radius of the eastern shore of Lake Tahoe, the Washoe silver mining activity promoted the central route across the Sierra more successfully than the recent convention. Now prospective railroad entrepreneurs were encouraged to build eastward by dreams of tapping the rich new trade.

Theodore D. Judah was one of the first to appreciate fully the affect of the silver strike on railroad affairs. Having come to California to be chief engineer of the Sacramento Valley Railroad, Judah soon became known for his dream of a railroad across the Sierra. From 1856 through the spring of 1859, he traveled between California and the East, lobbying in the halls of Congress and in eastern financial circles. Because of this experience, he had been chosen to take the Pacific Railroad Convention's resolutions to Congress. But Congress was in no mood to listen in 1860. Failure could not deter Judah. In the summer of 1860 he headed into the Sierra, pursuing a tip by Daniel Strong, doctor of Dutch Flat, who claimed that the best route across the Sierra passed through his community. By summer's end, Judah publicly announced that

Theodore D. Judah's dream of a Pacific Railroad at first gained
him notoriety, but later won him fame as a man of foresight
and constructive purpose. Judah persuaded Sacramento capitalists to create the Central Pacific Railroad, a corporation destined to become the western link of the first Pacific railroad. —
PIERCE FAMILY COLLECTION

Collis P. Huntington

Leland Stanford

Mark Hopkins

Charles Crocker

These four men, among the original stockholders of the Central Pacific Railroad, eventually came to dominate its operations, gaining the title *The Big Four.* — SOUTHERN PACIFIC COLLECTION

49

he and Strong, with the financial backing of Dutch Flat's citizenry, had found it — a route leading from Sacramento to Dutch Flat and on to Truckee, several miles north of Lake Tahoe. Angry that their chief engineer had broadcast his discovery in the press, the leadership of the Sacramento Valley Railroad dismissed him. But Judah was not discouraged. In November, he journeyed to San Francisco to interest the capitalists of the state's largest city in his idea, but there he met with no response. Not one to be defeated, he retreated to Sacramento, where he found enthusiastic support for his proposed route. By April 1861, a number of prominent Sacramento businessmen (including Leland Stanford, Collis Huntington, Mark Hopkins and Charles Crocker) had committed themselves to be stockholders in a company of which Judah would be chief engineer. The Central Pacific Railroad of California was formally incorporated under state law in June of that year.[1]

Sacramento's winter flood of 1861-62, seen by contemporaries as not wholly natural in origin, helped switch Sacramento's loyalties from the Sacramento Valley Railroad to the Central Pacific.

At the time of the new company's creation, Sacramento's local interests were primarily linked to the Sacramento Valley Railroad Company. That winter, however, the older company was blamed for a natural disaster in which Sacramento greatly suffered, an event which transferred the allegiance of its citizens to the Central Pacific. In December 1861, the waters of the American River burst the levies, flooding Sacramento. Outraged public opinion focused on the Sacramento Valley Railroad Company, whose embankments had kept the water in the city, thus promoting the flood. Moving to prevent a recurrence of these events, Sacramento's city government quickly passed an ordinance changing the route of the railroad into the city. Under the new law, the company's tracks would not be allowed to reach the Sacramento River, a provision strongly supported by Sacramento's draymen who would gain extra income from transporting goods from rail cars to ships. The company retaliated. Late in 1862, it announced that track would be laid to a new town, 16 miles down river from Sacramento. Called Freeport, the new terminal point would allow ship and rail car to come together, thus saving money for the shippers of the state. Through these developments, the Central Pacific became the sole champion of Sacramento's dreams of commercial empire.[2]

Cities that would not benefit from the Central Pacific's favored route joined the Sacramento Valley Railroad in opposition both to the new company and Sacramento. Placerville was one such community. Although traditionally associated with Sacramento in wagon road matters, Placerville was 35 miles south of Dutch Flat. Hence, the citizens of Placerville began to look toward Stockton as a possible new ally. The Pacific Railroad Convention's proposed route had favored Stockton, and the San Francisco and San Jose Railroad, a reorganized version of the defunct Pacific and Atlantic company, was building south from San Francisco along the convention's chosen route. Weighing these factors, Placerville decided to link her railroad hopes with those of San Francisco and Stockton, thus abandoning her old association with Sacramento.[3] By 1862, Sacramento was virtually left without an urban ally, unsuccessfully having attempted to tie neighboring communities such as Marysville to her commercial domain. Marysville's dream was to connect with Vallejo by rail while at the same time projecting

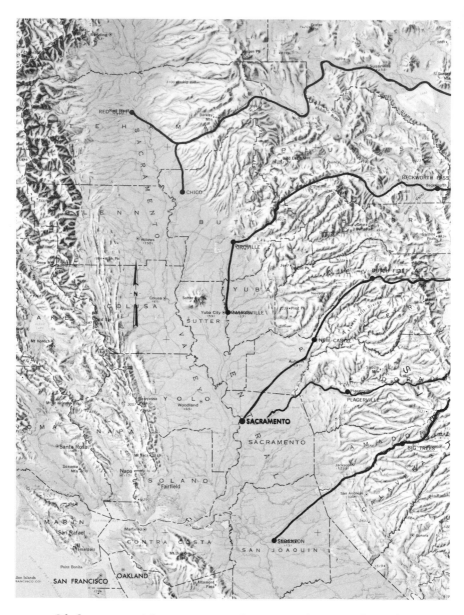

Of these potential routes across the Sierra, the Central Pacific
built along the Dutch Flat Route. The Sacramento Valley Railroad Company's line was completed to Folsom in 1856 and
was projected through to Placerville, which was almost reached
by the mid-1860's.

wagon and rail routes across the mountains to the silver mines. Offers of connecting with Sacramento were viewed with suspicion in Marysville. Comparing the possibilities of such a rail link to the construction of a line to Vallejo, a Marysville newspaper commented: "The latter is the sure guarantee of our city's prosperity, while the former is only a means of building up and benefiting Sacramento at our expense. No true friend to Marysville can hesitate in a case of this kind as to which enterprise he should foster and encourage."[4]

Although surrounded by urban rivals determined to direct the route of the first Pacific railroad away from Sacramento, the capital city never lost the initiative. Late in 1861, the Central Pacific sent Judah back to Washington to lobby for Sacramento's interests. Abraham Lincoln sat in the White House. Southern opponents to a central Pacific railroad had deserted Congress. Chances were good that Congress would deliver the long-awaited transcontinental railroad subsidy in 1862. And circumstances clearly favored Sacramento's Central Pacific. The first Republican president was bound by party interests to Leland Stanford, who had assumed the two roles of California's first Republican governor and president of the Central Pacific in 1861. The company's lobbyist was well known in the Capital because of his fervent efforts of the past. These advantages produced results. When the first Pacific Railroad Act passed in the summer of 1862, a key provision read:

> The Central Pacific Railroad Company of California, a Corporation existing under the laws of the State of California, are [sic] hereby authorized to construct a railroad and telegraph line from the Pacific coast, at or near San Francisco, or the navigable waters of the Sacramento river, to the eastern boundary of California.

The Union Pacific, a corporation created by the act, was authorized to build the rest of the line from a point on the Missouri River. Large land grants and generous federal loans were donated to both companies to speed construction.[5]

Sacramento and her railroad ally had won the prize of a federal subsidy. Likewise, the Central Pacific's directors felt fortunate in that they possessed the best route through the mountains. Judah had made cursory surveys of several Sierra routes but a thorough examination of only the one traversing Dutch Flat, which had several advantages over its rivals. It appeared to have the shortest snow line. Also, it crossed only one summit of the Sierra, whereas rival routes would encounter a double summit. And finally, it was one of the most direct lines from Sacramento to the Comstock silver mines in Nevada. The Central Pacific had definitely committed itself to the Dutch Flat route by the time of the passage of the act of 1862. Nevertheless, for months after that time the Sacramento managers of the road pretended no specific choice had been made, for they were aware that hostility and opposition of communities not benefited by their subsidized Dutch Flat route might prove materially damaging to their plans. Hence, they made newspaper advertisements, calling for information of other routes to be considered by the company. Supposedly after all information had been received, the route would be definitely chosen.[6] But this sham participation in the process of choosing the path across the mountains failed to produce the desired effect. For several years after the awarding of the Congressional prize to the Central Pacific, jealousy and opposition to the "Sacramento institution" was freely expressed in communities allied to other routes.

NOTES

1. Theodore D. Judah, *Report of Theodore D. Judah, Accredited Agent [of the] Pacific Railroad Convention, Upon his Operations in the Atlantic States* (San Francisco, 1860), pp. 6-7; *Committee on Railroads of the First Nevada Legislature. Evidence Concerning Projected Railways Across the Sierra Nevada Mountains* (Carson City, 1865), p. 205; *Daily Alta California,* Nov. 17, 1860, 2:1; Carl I. Wheat, "A Sketch of the Life of Theodore D. Judah," *California Historical Society Quarterly,* IV (1925), 227, 244-246; Helen Hinckley, *Rails from the West, A Biography of Theodore D. Judah* (San Marino, Calif., 1969), pp. 79-90.
2. William L. Willis, *History of Sacramento County, California* (Los Angeles, 1913), pp. 110-113; *Daily Alta California,* Dec. 17, 1861, 1:3; Dec. 23, 1861, 2:1; Dec. 21, 1862, 1:2.
3. *Daily Alta California,* April 12, 1862 (found in Bancroft Scraps [Bancroft Library, University of California, Berkeley], LXXX, 19-20); *ibid.,* Dec. 25, 1861, 1:7; Unidentified newspaper, Nov. 4, 1862 (found in Bancroft Scraps, LXVI, 28).
4. San Francisco and Marysville Railroad Co., *Reports of the Board of Directors and Chief Engineer* (Marysville, 1860), pp. 8, 26, 28, 39; *Sierra County News,* n.d. (found in Bancroft Scraps, LXVI, 6); Marysville newspaper reprinted in *Daily Alta California,* Oct. 6, 1859, 1:6.

5. George Clark, *Leland Stanford (1824-1893): War Governor of California, Railroad Builder and Founder of Stanford University* (Stanford, 1931), p. 176; Margaret H. Mudgett, "The Political Career of Leland Stanford" (Master's thesis, University of Southern California, 1933), pp. 5, 14; *Testimony Taken by the United States Pacific Railway Commission, Appointed Under the Act of Congress Approved March 3, 1887* (Washington, 1887), V, 2842; *Congressional Globe,* 37 Cong., 2 sess. (appendix), pp. 381-384.
6. While the snow along the line was at times very deep, it was predicted that the length of track obstructed by winter snow would be only a short distance; *Testimony Taken by the United States Pacific Railway Commission,* V, 2618; Chester L. White, "Surmounting the Sierras, The Campaign for a Wagon Road," *California Historical Society Quarterly,* VII (1928), 8; Clark, *Leland Stanford,* pp. 171-172; Committee on Railroads of the First Nevada Legislature, *Evidence,* p. 12.

Projected by the directors of the Central Pacific, the Dutch
Flat Wagon Road became the *cause celebre* of the company's
opponents. The furor over the wagon road's construction ham-
pered the progress of the Central Pacific eastward. — DONALD
DUKE COLLECTION

5

Obstruction

A torrent of verbal abuse poured down upon Sacramento in the fall of 1862. Sacramentans, it was charged, had always exhibited "the most intense selfishness to obtain all works of a public nature to be located in their city." First, they had secured the state's capital and then had captured control of the western end of the great Pacific railroad for "their exclusive use and profit." Concerned citizens were disturbed by "the indecent haste and unscrupulous desire of Sacramentans to usurp to themselves all the advantages of a Pacific Railroad to pass through their city, to the unjust exclusion of other portions of the State." To many, the Central Pacific's success in Congress merely manifested Sacramento's long-standing "greedy, grasping propensities to hold the reins, to whip and spur at pleasure." "By dexterous conduct at Washington" and not by the proven worth of their chosen route, a few Sacramentans had manipulated the subsidy bill through Congress, unaccompanied by any guarantee that the route selected by the Central Pacific would "result in the common benefit of the whole people."[1]

Placerville's denizens were especially vocal in disputing the superiority of Sacramento's Dutch Flat route. Challenging Judah's claim that his route had the shortest snow line, the mountain town's backers observed bitterly that the tragic Donner party of 1846 had been trapped in heavy snows along the proposed survey. Judah, they claimed, lied in saying that he had examined the Placerville route. Most inhabitants of Nevada territory joined Placerville in attacking Judah's route, for it would enter their territory far north of the silver mining area's principal towns. A railroad built by way of Placerville would be more to their liking. Some even demanded that the Pacific Railroad Act be amended to require that the line pass through Carson City.[2]

The *Marysville Appeal* joined the fray. "There are certain considerations of practicability which are more powerful than local desires," noted its editor in proclaiming the superiority of Marysville's favored route across the mountains via Beckwourth's Pass. Forty miles north of Judah's survey, Beckwourth's Pass was proclaimed to have less snow than any comparable place in the Sierra. Had Judah not "owned a town site on the selected line of railway," the newspaper charged, he would not have made a similar claim for his route. Only the crutch of government subsidy could induce capitalists to build over so treacherous a journey. These accusations were not ignored in Sacramento. The press of that city replied that the canyon of the middle fork of the Feather River along the Marysville route was narrow, extremely crooked and "one of the most fearful man ever looked upon." Marysville's partisans retorted that it was "a very commonplace canyon and as well-known and easily traversed as any other mining stream in the State." Marysville would fail at this time to win the struggle for her route. However, 50 years later a transcontinental line would enter California through Beckwourth's Pass, justifying to many citizens of Marysville the correctness of their earlier claims.[3]

About the only way the Central Pacific could have avoided these locally inspired complaints and attacks would have been to announce that its route would meander through the central part of the state, thus benefiting every small village. Indeed, such an idea was seriously suggested, but nothing came of it, for the Central Pacific was required by the act of 1862 to build upon the "most direct, central, and practicable route" across the Sierra. As Leland Stanford later noted, such opposition was "necessarily incident to the construction of the Pacific Railroad."[4]

Powerful corporations were often tied to localities hostile to the Central Pacific. All railroad companies projected to serve communities rivaling Sacramento helped finance the barrage of propaganda against the "Sacramento institution." Likewise, all stage coach lines engaged in the transmontane traffic, together with wagon road toll companies, contributed to the opposition, a key example of the latter being the wagon road connecting Placerville with Nevada Territory. The California State Telegraph Company, the western link of the first transcontinental telegraph line, also had good reason to fight the progress of the Central Pacific. This company, whose wires traveled eastward via Placerville, feared competition from the telegraph line which the Pacific Railroad Act required the Central Pacific and the Union Pacific to build.

Other concerns, not necessarily tied to local interests, joined the anti-Central Pacific forces. The California Steam Navigation Company, plying the rivers of the state, sought to delay active railroad competition, as did the Pacific Mail Steamship Company in transcontinental traffic. Other firms, like the Sitka Ice Company, feared obliteration of their businesses once the railroad crossed the mountains. Ice for California markets could be more cheaply procured in the Sierra than along the northern Pacific coast. Many local manufacturers also feared competition of less expensive eastern goods, if and when the Pacific railroad was completed.[5]

Some of these concerns were tied to each other in interesting ways. Wells, Fargo & Company, which engaged in the carrying trade over the Placerville route, lent large sums to an affiliate of the Sacramento Valley Railroad attempting to connect its parent company and Placerville with the Washoe mines. The presidents of Wells, Fargo and the San Francisco and Washoe Railroad, as the affiliate was called, were brothers, indicating that more than just financial ties bound the two firms. J. Mora Moss, president of the Sitka Ice Company, was both a power in the Sacramento Valley Railroad and a director of the California State Telegraph Company.[6] Frederick MacCrellish, another director of the telegraph company, also served as publisher of the *Alta California,* a San Francisco newspaper noted for its hostility to the Central Pacific in the early sixties. But perhaps the most interesting interlocking relationship among opponents of the Central Pacific involved a

French banking firm, named Pioche and Bayerque, and the Sacramento Valley Railroad. As the primary financial backer of the latter company, Pioche and Bayerque kept alive the most active opposition of the Sacramento Valley Railroad to the Central Pacific. This banking house, it was charged before the Nevada senate in 1865, was "devoted to the interests of the French Emperor."

> He has cast a covetous eye upon Mexico, and has apparently succeeded in placing his minion, Maximillian, in power. He has evidently expected that the rebellion of the Southern traitors would end in the dismemberment of the Great Republic, and that event he undoubtedly expected, would open the way for the conquest of California, on the plea that it was never rightfully separated from Mexico. The construction of the Pacific Railroad, by bringing the Atlantic and Pacific States closer together, would, of course, defeat all such schemes.[7]

Hence, not all opposition to the Central Pacific was born from local rivalries, but certainly most of the rhetoric hostile to the company reflected the local jealousies of the day. Because concerns with other motives exploited such attitudes to further their own ends, it is difficult to guage the genuine intensity of local feeling on railroad affairs in the early 1860's. Nevertheless, the very fact that the language of debate was usually couched in those terms helped indicate the current climate of opinion. The readers of newspapers and hearers of speeches would respond to such vendettas.

A good example of corporate and community interests combining to battle the Central Pacific's progress was the working alliance between Placerville and the Sacramento Valley Railroad and its previously mentioned affiliate. The latter companies were intending to build a line to Nevada via Placerville. If the Central Pacific won the race across the mountains, they would lose most of their trade, except for that around Placerville. Likewise, Placerville's dreams of becoming a commercial emporium would be dashed. Hence the community, and the railroad identified with it, fought the Central Pacific without quarter. In the California legislature and then in the Nevada Constitutional Convention of 1864, they drafted, presented, and lobbied for propositions to award several million dollars to the railroad company which would first reach the California-Nevada line. If passed, both measures would have weakened the Central Pacific while strengthening its Placerville-oriented rivals in domestic and foreign money markets. To the relief of Stanford and his colleagues, both proposals were defeated.[8]

But that was not the end of trouble for the Central Pacific. In the summer of 1864, the company's directors completed the Dutch Flat wagon road, which was to serve as a temporary connection between their eastward building railroad and the Nevada mines. Rate and service competition with Placerville's rival wagon road immediately commenced. Trials of speed were held, with proponents of both routes claiming victory. Passengers appeared to prefer the more scenic journey via Placerville, while teamsters and shippers of freight favored the wider Dutch Flat road. Other forms of competition were not as peaceful. In late April, gangs of rowdies backed by Sacramento city authorities and the Central Pacific began ripping out the Sacramento Valley Railroad's track in the city

DUTCH FLAT WAGON ROAD.

This new route over the Mountains, by way of Dutch Flat and Donner Lake, can now be traveled by Teams without load, and will be open for loaded Teams

JUNE 15th, 1864.

IT IS

The Shortest, Best and Cheapest Route to Washoe, Humboldt and Reese River.

Its grade going East at no place exceeds ten inches to the rod, and it is wide enough for Two Teams to pass without difficulty. All teams coming West, without load, can travel the New Road FREE OF TOLL until further notice. All those taking loads at Newcastle, the terminus of the Central Pacific Railroad, three miles from Auburn, can travel the New Road going East, Free of Toll, up to July 1, 1864.

Teams starting from Virginia City will take the Henness Pass Road to Ingram's, at Sardine Valley, where the New Road turns off to the left.

CHARLES CROCKER.

Sacramento, June 6, 1864   Pres't of the Co.

in violation of a court order. More violence between the two companies occurred several months later at Auburn in Placer county when the Sacramento Valley Railroad began tearing up the track connecting that community with its main line. The track removal squad, intending to use the rails for the extension to Placerville, was physically opposed by a mob composed of Auburn's citizens and hired toughs of the Central Pacific. Even so, the Sacramento Valley line was the victor in this skirmish.[9]

However, the war was ultimately won by the Central Pacific. In the summer of 1864 Congress passed a second Pacific Railroad Act, doubling the land grant and easing the financial burden of the two transcontinental railroad companies. "The financial problem has been solved," rejoiced Leland Stanford. The firms allied with Placerville could not match such assistance, and the following year the Sacramento Valley Railroad was sold cheaply to the victors. Soon thereafter, the track connecting Freeport with the purchased line was removed and one threat to Sacramento was no more.[10]

Before the passage of the Act of 1864, even Placerville's efforts at obstruction were overshadowed by those of San Francisco. The city's opposition was rooted in the fact of the Central Pacific's ties to Sacramento. The company's subscription books had first opened in the latter town in 1862 to help insure that the firm's control would remain in Sacramento. Fully realizing the importance of this opportunity, one Sacramento newspaper had urged the community to take advantage of it: "As a matter of local pride as well as for the promotion of self-interest, every citizen of Sacramento ought to encourage the enterprise by subscribing for stock. As far as possible it should be made a Sacramento institution."[11] Sacramento eagerly seized the chance. Later, the subscription books were taken to San Francisco, where the failure of the company to attract support was quite noticeable. Many explanations have been given to explain the reluctance of bay city residents to back the enterprise. They were supposedly not public spirited; but to the contrary, they had shown an active interest in railroad affairs. Because of their efforts, the Pacific Railroad Convention had been held in San Francisco in 1859. Because of their energy in the convention, San Francisco had been selected as the western terminus by the delegates. In the early 1860's, they were supporting, privately and publicly, the San Francisco and San Jose Railroad, which originally they had viewed as the first link of the Pacific railroad.

Supposedly San Francisco's capitalists refused to support the Central Pacific because the immediate returns of such action would be paltry when compared to those of other investments. But other explanations can also be given. First of all, moneyed San Franciscans were wary of investing in a corporation tightly controlled by a group of Sacramentans. Secondly, many of San Francisco's leading capitalists were interested in railroad enterprises and other concerns rivaling the Central Pacific. They certainly could not be expected to lend aid to their enemy. Likewise, those San Franciscans actively interested in railroad affairs were committed to routes other than the one projected by the Sacramento company. This commitment was clearly reflected in a letter to the editor of the *Alta California,* describing the Central Pacific as "merely a branch or side cut for the benefit of Sacramento, as it is not necessary for a Pacific Railroad direct from this city to go to within thirty-five miles of that place."[12]

Finally, the question of the terminus of the Pacific railroad bothered San Franciscans. In July 1862, San Franciscans had ecstatically rejoiced upon hearing that Congress had agreed to subsidize a central transcontinental railroad. A torchlight procession was held, the parade route decorated with numerous banners, some of which read: "San Francisco — The completion of the Atlantic and Pacific Railroad will make San Francisco the King City of the World!" "San Francisco, the jumping-off depot!" But later, upon carefully reading the act of Congress, bay city residents found cause to question their enthusiasm, for unlike the recommendations of the Pacific Railroad Convention of 1859 the bill did not make San Francisco the terminus. Under the vague language of the act, San Francisco, Sacramento, or any place in between could become "the jumping-off depot." The choice was left to the Central Pacific. San Franciscans felt cheated and blamed Sacramento schemers for the result. The Central Pacific was quick to reject charges of duplicity, claiming that the ambiguities of the bill had been included to insure its passage. Fence-sitting congressmen, it claimed, could be persuaded to subsidize the project only as far as Sacramento, the first major city west of the Sierra. Thus, it was argued, the language relating to the terminus was framed to gain the support of these legislators. Such an explanation was not acceptable to many San Franciscans. They recalled that Sacramento's delegates had unsuccessfully fought for a similar vague provision in the Pacific Railroad Convention of 1859. "Have the conclusions arrived at by the Pacific Railroad Convention turned out to be mere subterfuge; or has political stockjobbing taken precedence?" asked a letter to the editor of the *Alta California*.[13]

Certainly Sacramento's press did little to calm the fear and frustration rising in San Francisco. Noting that the Sacramento River connected San Francisco with the capital city, the *Sacramento Union* argued that it would be foolish to begin construction of the Pacific railroad in San Francisco. "Hence," concluded one *Union* editorial, "we assume that this city is the point where the work on the Pacific Railroad should be commenced." Some were so bold as to predict that Sacramento would be the line's permanent terminus, not just a temporary one. Located in the center of the state, Sacramento was a natural site from which railroads would one day radiate. Other great cities of the world were located inland — Paris, Brussels, Berlin, to name a few. Sacramento, it was prophesied, would follow their example. San Francisco would be dwarfed in the process. But perhaps nature would intervene with a tremendous earthquake to save the bay city's citizens from suffering undue humiliation, allowing San Francisco to "sink into the bottom of the sea, as did Callao in 1746."[14]

Sacramento's bombast understandably angered San Franciscans who waited nervously during the fall of 1862 for some definite word on the terminus. The Central Pacific would start construction in Sacramento; that was apparent. But a rumor that Theodore Judah had promised the San Francisco and San Jose Railroad Company federal aid to build between San Francisco and Sacramento kept the bay city astir. The promise had been made while Judah was working for the passage of the act of 1862 in Washington, D.C. If honored, the pledge would make San Francisco the terminus of the Pacific railroad, but months went by with tight silence by the Central Pacific. Needing the city's support, the company ultimately publicly reaffirmed its promise. In December 1862, the owners of the San Francisco and San Jose road incorporated the Western Pacific to build from San Jose to Sacramento, via Stockton, and the Central Pacific assigned both San Francisco firms to receive government aid. San Francisco rejoiced, but with a reserve that comes with uncertainty. Because of ambiguities in the Pacific Railroad Act, many doubted that the Central Pacific had the power to grant a federal subsidy to the projected line between San Francisco and Sacramento. It soon became apparent that without a specific amendment by Congress, no aid would be forthcoming; and not until March 3, 1865, would the necessary bill be passed. In short, despite the Central Pacific's verbal pledge, San Francisco was still "out in the cold."[15] Thus, the Sacramento company remained an object of distrust in the bay city.

Meanwhile, under the prodding hand of Governor Stanford, the state legislature passed several bills authorizing San Francisco, Sacramento, and Placer counties* to subsidize the Central Pacific. Certainly Placer and Sacramento counties would consent to aiding the company, for both would be served by the Dutch Flat route. But since San Francisco was less likely to approve, the company's backers drafted the San Francisco subsidy bill also to include generous aid to the Western Pacific, a corporation with wide support in San Francisco. To the rue of many bay city residents, the two propositions were indivisible. The vote would be either for or against the two. If the subscription passed, the city would buy $600,000 of the Central Pacific's stock and $400,000 of the Western Pacific's.[16]

In the San Francisco election, more than the subsidy money was at stake. Eastern and foreign capitalists had to be convinced that the Sacramento firm was a reliable security before they would invest, and a favorable vote from California's leading city would be persuasive to that end. Hence, the company allowed no chances for failure. It instituted a campaign to persuade the workingmen of the city that a "yes" vote would mean more jobs in railroad construction. There are also indications that Central Pacific agents stooped to mass bribery on election day. When the votes were

*Placer county should not be confused with Placerville, which is in El Dorado county.

counted the subsidy had been won by a two to one margin, but San Francisco's leading citizens refused to acquiesce gracefully in the Central Pacific's victory. They openly charged Leland Stanford's brother with scattering money among the "wharf rats" of the city to carry the election. They accused the company's managers of deliberately pursuing a policy that would bankrupt the company while enriching themselves. They pointed to the Central Pacific directors' granting of the contract to build the road to a construction firm owned by themselves, without competitive bidding. They warned that if the railroad company went bankrupt by such schemes, all stockholders, including the city of San Francisco, would be liable up to the full extent of their resources, for California offered investors no limited liability protection.[17]

These San Francisco enemies of the company released a barrage of propaganda which they hoped would cripple its progress. The Central Pacific, they claimed, was in reality the "Dutch Flat Swindle." This charge was born from the fact that in 1861, the principal Sacramento merchants backing the enterprise had formed a separate concern, the Dutch Flat and Donner Lake Wagon Road Company. Their reason for this action was that they then doubted that the necessary finances could be raised to build over the most rugged portion of their chosen route, between Dutch Flat and the Nevada mines, which could be traversed by their inexpensive wagon road. In any case, Washoe's silver could be shipped westward, insuring the transportation entrepreneurs profit even if the railroad fell short. Arguments that this was wise contingency planning had little effect. The Central Pacific's enemies saw the wagon road as proof that the company had no intention of building a transcontinental railroad, and instead was only bilking both the federal government and its other supporters in order to build a spur to serve its directors' wagon road. With this vision in mind, wags concocted new names for the railroad company: "the so-called Central Pacific Railroad," "the local Central Pacific," "the railroad running from nowhere to nowhere." When castigated for attempting to kill the goose that would lay the golden egg, they retorted that the Dutch Flat scheme was not a goose but rather a "lame duck."[18]

They also damned the Central Pacific for having "totally ignored all present vested interests." In other words, the company had refused to buy out the Sacramento Valley Railroad and instead began constructing a rival line into the mountains. Even though the Central Pacific explained that the Sacramento Valley road was overcapitalized and was constructed with light rails, and that the Central Pacific could receive no federal aid toward the purchase of the line, the chorus of opposition continued to rise.[19]

Members of San Francisco's Board of Supervisors, openly hostile to the firm, were refused the opportunity to review the financial workings of the Central Pacific on the grounds that injury to the enterprise was their sole motivation. This rebuff, coupled with Judah's departure from the company, led the supervisors to conclude publicly that the Central Pacific was corrupt, as had long been charged. Shortly thereafter, Judah succumbed to a tropical illness, and the reasons for his quarrel with the directors died with him. But rumors persisted that this honest man had discovered corruption and could not live with it. Petitions calling for open books were circulated, but the directors were unyielding, and the secrets were kept.[20]

Nevertheless, wealthy San Franciscans continued to complain loudly of being "taxed for a state road whose terminus is a hundred miles from the [municipal] corporation taxed, and whose advantages are merely incidental." Visiting the bay city at the height of the anti-Central Pacific agitation, a *Sacramento Union* reporter wrote: "The people here are easily excited, and pray for the downfall of Sacramento, as well as Richmond." Backed by such hostility, suits were initiated to legally prevent the delivery of San Francisco's bonds to the Central Pacific. Finally, after lengthy legal battles, a settlement was reached. Because of the city government's expressed fear of unlimited liability, San Francisco was allowed to donate $400,000 as a gift to the corporation, in lieu of the $600,000 purchase of company stock.[21]

Meanwhile, as the San Francisco enemies of the Central Pacific raged, most of the state's legislators realized that such opposition would be detrimental to the best interests of the state. Bills authorizing county subsidies and those granting state aid passed in rapid succession in the sessions of 1863 and 1864. And the result was achieved with little or no corruption by the Central Pacific.

67

J. Mora Moss   **Frederick MacCrellish**

They led San Francisco's opposition to the Central Pacific in
the early 1860's, using the weapons of publicity, politics, and
finance. — WRIGHTWOOD COLLECTION

One political opponent of the company a decade later aptly described the essence of state-wide railroad politics in the early 1860's:
"No man's political reputation was worth anything who opposed
the granting of railroad subsidies. It was the all-important subject."
The majority of Californians at this time were not the merchants,
farmers, and entrepreneurs opposing the Central Pacific because of
local and business interests. They were the common people who
dreamed of easier communications with their families in the East.
They did not see their interests tied to any particular community.
They were poor people who would not bear the tax burden of lav-
ish subsidies. And they were voters who would withdraw support
from politicians hostile to the Central Pacific. In this political atmosphere, corruption was unnecessary. Even anti-railroad organs
would later recall that the company's corruption of politics did
not begin until 1868.[22]

Despite the subsidy bills of friendly legislatures, opponents of
the Sacramento institution could and did use the courts to delay
the issuing of state and local bonds. But in almost every suit the
Central Pacific emerged the victor, thanks in part to state supreme
court Justice E. B. Crocker, brother of one of the company's directors and an appointee of Governor Stanford. Ironically, San

Franciscans ultimately injured their own local interests by their legal delaying tactics. During 1863 and 1864, unusually mild winters allowed for swift construction in the Sierra. But during these years, the company received no federal loans, and state and local aid, such as San Francisco's, was being contested in court. Lacking funds, the Central Pacific was unable to take advantage of nature's reprieve, and construction had to stop at Newcastle, 31 miles from Sacramento. Years later, Leland Stanford recalled the lost opportunity: "Except for the delay consequent upon this opposition, we would more easily have met the Union Pacific at Cheyenne than we did at Promontory. . . . It would have given to San Francisco complete control of the business of Utah, Wyoming, Montana, and Idaho." Eastern cities came to control this trade, because some San Franciscans and other Californians viewing the Central Pacific as a "Sacramento institution" failed to foresee how the realities of railroad economics would operate upon a transcontinental line without rail competition. This they would learn later.[23]

When the Central Pacific Railroad crossed the Sierra, the Dutch Flat Wagon Road lost its reason for existing. — DONALD DUKE COLLECTION

NOTES

1. *San Francisco Bulletin,* Jan. (day unknown), 1863 (found in Bancroft Scraps [Bancroft Library, University of California, Berkeley], LXXX, 1056); unidentified Stockton newspaper, Jan. 8, 1861 (found in Bancroft Scraps, LXXX, 15-16); *Daily Alta California,* Sept. 3, 1862 (found in Bancroft Scraps, LXXX, 640-641); *San Francisco Bulletin,* Oct. 4, 1862 (found in Bancroft Scraps, LXXX, 640); *Daily Alta California,* Nov. 20, 1862, 1:3.
2. *Daily Alta California,* Nov. 26, 1862, 1:2; Dec. 22, 1862, 1:2; July 17, 1862, 1:7; Nov. 17, 1862, 1:2.
3. George C. Mansfield, *History of Butte County, California* (Los Angeles, 1918), p. 249; *Marysville Appeal,* Oct.1 8, 1862 (found in Bancroft Scraps, LXXX, 637); *ibid.,* date unknown (found in Bancroft Scraps, LXXX, 981-982); *Sacramento Union,* date unknown (found in Bancroft Scraps, LXXX, 982-983); *San Francisco Bulletin,* Nov. 23, 1862 (found in Bancroft Scraps, LXXX, 1052).
4. Committee on Railroads of the First Nevada Legislature, *Evidence Concerning Projected Railroads Across the Sierra Nevada Mountains* (Carson City, Nev., 1865), pp. 12-13; *Daily Alta California,* Nov. 12, 1862, 1:4-5; *Sacramento Union,* Nov. 24, 1862 (found in Bancroft Scraps, LXXX, 1052).
5. Timothy Hopkins, Random Notes on Central Pacific History, 1885 (manuscript at Hopkins Transportation Library, Stanford California), pp. 3-5.
6. Unidentified newspaper, Jan. (day unknown), 1869 (found in Bancroft Scraps, LXXX, 131); James McCague, *Moguls and Iron Men. The Story of the First Transcontinental Railroad* (New York, 1964), pp. 52, 79; *Daily Alta California,* June 21, 1865, 1:6; Hubert Howe Bancroft, *History of the Life of Leland Stanford, A Character Study* (Oakland, 1952), p. 38; *Daily Alta California,* Nov. 7, 1861, 2:1.
7. Hon. N. W. Winton, *Pacific Railroad Speech in the Nevada Senate, Feb. 27, 1865* (Carson City, Nev., 1865), pp. 12-13.
8. *Daily Alta California,* Mar. 6, 1864, 2:1; Thomas H. Thompson and Albert A. West, *History of Nevada,* 1881 (Berkeley, 1958: reprint), pp. 274-275.
9. *The Pacific Railroad, A Defense Against Its Enemies, With Report of the Supervisors of Placer County, and Report of of Mr. Montanya* (San Francisco, 1864), p. 20; *Daily Alta California,* April 24, 1864, 2:1; Oct. 16, 1864, 2:2; Jan. 31, 1865, 1:3; unidentified newspaper, July 12, 1862 (found in Bancroft Scraps, LXVI, 25); William L. Willis, *History of Sacramento County, California* (Los Angeles, 1913), pp. 195-196.
10. *Congressional Globe,* 38 Cong., 1 sess. (appendix), pp. 250-253; Hubert Howe Bancroft, *History of California* (San Francisco, 1890), VII, 565-566; Willis, *Sacramento County,* pp. 195-196.
11. Unidentified Sacramento newspaper, month and day unknown, 1862 (found in Bancroft Scraps, LXXX, 641); Bancroft, *Life of Leland Stanford,* p. 36.
12. James McCague, *Moguls and Iron Men,* pp. 18-19; *Daily Alta California,* April 3, 1863, 1:3; April 4, 1863, 1:3; Jan. 5, 1864, 1:3; David Lavender, *The Great Persuader* (New York, 1970), p. 91.
13. *San Francisco Bulletin,* Nov. 4, 1862 (found in Bancroft Scraps, LXXX, 645-646); *Daily Alta California,* July 11, 1862, 1:1-2; Nov. 5, 1862, 2:2.
14. *Sacramento Union,* Nov. 6, 1862 (found in Bancroft Scraps, LXXX, 1047); *Knight's Landing News,* date unknown (found in Bancroft Scraps, LXXX, 630-631); *Sacramento Union* quoted in *Daily Alta California,* Oct. 28, 1866, 1:7; *Sacramento Bee* quoted in *Daily Alta California,* Jan. 1, 1863.
15. *Testimony Taken by the United States Pacific Railway Commission, Appointed Under the Act of Congress Approved March 3, 1887* (Washington,

1887), I, 12; *Sacramento Bee,* month and day unknown, 1862 (found in Bancroft Scraps, LXXX, 8); *San Francisco Bulletin,* Dec. 20, 1862 (found in Bancroft Scraps, LXXX, 647-648); *Daily Alta California,* May 17, 1863, 1:3; July 8, 1864, 2:1; *San Diego Union,* Jan. (day unknown), 1866 (found in Bancroft Scraps, LXXX, 663).

16. *Daily Alta California,* May 2, 1863, 1:1; April 17, 1863, 1:3.

17. "Governor's Annual Message," *Journal of the California Assembly, 15th Session* (Sacramento, 1864), pp. 57-58; *Daily Alta California,* Jan. 29, 1863, 1:3; May 21, 1863, 1:2-3; May 25, 1863, 1:1; Feb. 8, 1864, 2:1; *The Great Dutch Flat Swindle! The City of San Francisco Demands Justice! The Matter in Controversy, and the Present State of the Question, An Address to the Board of Supervisors, Officers and People of San Francisco* (San Francisco, 1864), p. 60.

18. *Daily Alta California,* Dec. 7, 1863, 1:3, Feb. 16, 1865, 2:1; Feb. 20, 1865, 2:1.

19. Committee on Railroads of the First Nevada Legislature, *Evidence,* p. 150; Carl I. Wheat, "A Sketch of the Life of Theodore D. Judah," *California Historical Society Quarterly,* IV (1925), 258-259.

20. *The Pacific Railroad, A Defense Against Its Enemies,* pp. 11-12; Collis P. Huntington later remembered Judah as a man of "low, thieving cunning" with a "large amount of cheap dignity." See *Letters from Collis P. Huntington to Mark Hopkins, Leland Stanford, Charles Crocker, E. B. Crocker, Charles F. Crocker, and David D. Colton* (New York, 1892-1894), I, 188; *Daily Alta California,* Aug. 13, 1864, 1:6.

21. *The Great Dutch Flat Swindle!,* p. 39; *Sacramento Union* quoted in *Daily Alta California,* Dec. 15, 1864, 1:1; June 21, 1864, 1:3; April 11, 1865, 1:3.

22. *Debates and Proceedings of the Constitutional Convention of the State of California, Convened at the City of Sacramento, Saturday, September 28, 1878* (Sacramento, 1881), I, 573; *San Francisco Chronicle,* Aug. 17, 1879 (found in Bancroft Scraps, LXXX, 882); Theodore H. Hittell, *History of California* (San Francisco, 1898), IV, 467-468.

23. *Testimony Taken by the United States Pacific Railway Commission,* VI, 3610-3611; Thompson and West, *History of Nevada, 1881,* p. 273; Wesley S. Griswold, *A Work of Giants: Building the First Transcontinental Railroad* (New York, 1962), pp. 92-93.

The great curved trestle at Secret Town was the largest structure of its type on the Central Pacific. It was a combination of engineering skill and Chinese labor that took the Central Pacific eastward across the Sierra. — SOUTHERN PACIFIC COLLECTION

6

Race for
Commercial Empire

A T its inception, the westward-building Union Pacific was not
clearly identified with any particular community as was its
western counterpart. The act of 1862 had stated that the eastern
company was to begin construction somewhere on the hundreth
meridian between the Republican and Platte Rivers; in short, "out
in the middle of nowhere." Various branch lines were to be built
to connect this lonely outpost with larger communities along the
Missouri River, one of which was to be designated the official
eastern terminus by the President of the United States. These provisions clearly reflected the intensity of local pressures on Congress, which had transferred the final choice to the President.
Delegations from Missouri River towns descended on Lincoln in
the spring of 1863, each claiming to have superior advantages as
a terminal facility. Not until November did Lincoln name Omaha
as the winner.[1]

With this time-absorbing problem solved, the Union Pacific
had to face other obstacles. No railroad connected the Mississippi
River with Omaha. All supplies and materials had to be transported westward over the Missouri River, choked with ice in the
winter and partially obstructed with sand bars in summer. In addition, few capitalists could be persuaded to invest in the company,

for unlike the Central Pacific, it held no promise of developing a rich local trade. And so nothing was accomplished by the company until the act of 1864 made it a more attractive financial investment. Construction then began. In grading the first 20 miles, the Union Pacific's engineers decided to alter slightly the course projected earlier, and localities along the old route protested vigorously, delaying governmental authorization of the change for four months. By January of 1866 only 40 miles had been laid on the Union Pacific's line in comparison with the 60 miles on the more rugged Dutch Flat route.[2]

The Central Pacific's superior rate of progress had its effect in Washington. Initially, Congress had thought that the Union Pacific would meet the Central Pacific near the eastern boundary of California, for it then believed that the Sierra Nevada mountains would be the greatest obstacle to overcome. However, by 1864 Congress was more knowledgeable of the problems delaying the Union Pacific's construction, and so authorized the Central Pacific to build 150 miles into Nevada. Two years later, still another change was made, when Congress removed this limitation upon the more energetic California company. The two companies would build until they met. A race for empire was thus inaugurated.[3]

With visions of a great prize before them, even former local enemies rallied to the standard of the Central Pacific. In their minds, the Sacramento institution had suddenly become a California enterprise. The *Alta California,* an old opponent of the Central Pacific, reflected this change in attitude:

> The Pacific Railroad is no longer a wild dream or an untrustworthy promise. . . . Peculiar influences are driving the work ahead at both ends. In the first place Congress has provided each company shall have as much of the road as it can build; so that the company which advances with most rapidity gets the most. And the trade of the interior of the continent makes it of vast importance to get as much as possible.

It was more than a race between railroad companies, vying for federal land grants and financial assistance. For many Californians, it was a contest between cities, with San Francisco pitted against Chicago and St. Louis, and Sacramento contending with Omaha and Council Bluffs. San Francisco merchants now foresaw that the

Laying its early miles of track in mountainous terrain, Central Pacific work crews endured great hardships. Before 1866, they had laid more miles of track than the westward building Union Pacific. In this scene, locomotive No. 11, the *Arctic*, brings passenger service to the railhead in Dixie Cut, near Blue Canyon. — HUNTINGTON LIBRARY, SAN MARINO, CALIFORNIA

A construction train in Truckee River Canyon, the orphaned section of the railroad, before the Summit Tunnel was completed. — HUNTINGTON LIBRARY, SAN MARINO, CALIFORNIA

Central Pacific would discriminate in their favor and against eastern merchants in order to maximize long haul traffic over its part of the line. The Union Pacific would operate in a similar manner to benefit the merchants of the Mississippi Valley. In effect, the meeting place of the two roads would draw the boundary line of San Francisco's commercial empire. Hence, local jealousies within California were temporarily shelved, as local rivalries on a continental scale captured the imaginations of California's urban imperialists.[4]

Meeting the challenge of the California company, the Union Pacific out-constructed its rival in 1866 and 1867, completing 550 miles of track by the end of 1867, while the Central Pacific could boast of only 136 miles of railroad over the rugged Sierra. However, the Union Pacific had yet to encounter the Rocky Mountains. In the summer of 1867, Collis Huntington was confidently predicting that his company would connect with the Union Pacific 100 miles east of the Great Salt Lake. But discouraging events continually assaulted this optimism. The fierce winter of 1866-1867 slowed the Central Pacific's progress in the high Sierra, but a liberal use of powder and cash resulted in gains even during this period. After the spring thaw, a new problem arose when the company's Chinese workers struck for higher pay. Charles Crocker, directing the construction, skillfully broke the protest by plying the orientals with threats and promises, and the work continued. Significantly, Crocker blamed the whole affair on Union Pacific agitators. In this contest, few holds were barred.[5]

As the gap between the contending construction gangs diminished, rumors arose that the Union Pacific might pass its rival in the Utah desert and build to Vallejo. It was public knowledge that a survey of the Beckwourth Pass route into California was in the possession of the Union Pacific, and this had a two-fold effect. First of all, these rumors weakened the desire of capitalists to invest in the Central Pacific, which would be seriously injured by a competitive line. They also rekindled the local aspirations of Marysville

An Indian at the top of the Palisades in Nevada gazes down on the Central Pacific tracks. In Nevada, the railroad got its first real opportunity for speedy construction. — ROBERT WEINSTEIN COLLECTION

and Vallejo. "When they pass the Central Pacific tracklayers and continue to run westward with an independent line, little doubt will be left in the general mind about the near greatness of our town," crowed the editor of a Vallejo newspaper. Chico and Susanville also joined the northern California chorus for the Union Pacific, advising that the proper entrance for the company was through Noble's Pass, north of the Marysville route. The facade of united local support for the Central Pacific was broken. The next salvo in this war of rumors and words belonged to Leland Stanford, who announced to the press in December 1868 that the Central Pacific would build its own line to the Missouri River, because of the impassibility of the Union Pacific's road in winter. Although the Central Pacific never followed through on its threat and the Union Pacific would wait until the 1880's to construct an extension to the Pacific coast, these rumors were slow to die.[6]

Meanwhile, both companies vied for influence with federal officials, whose regulation of route selections and control of the government's financial aid made them significant in the struggle. Following a rare defeat at the hands of these officials, Collis Hunt-

Nevada's obstacle was its aridity. Water was one principal commodity shipped from Winnemucca, to end of track, so that construction could continue. — GERALD M. BEST COLLECTION

J. H. Strobridge, in the dark suit, stands in the center of a flat car at Rozel after setting the record-breaking feat of laying 10 miles of track in one day. Note camp cars and tents in the upper right of the illustration. — SOUTHERN PACIFIC COLLECTION

ington wrote to his western companions, "The Union Pacific has evidently outbid me." In another instance, he wrote his friends that he was willing to bribe the Secretary of Interior with $100,000 to get him to aid his company's efforts to meet the Union Pacific at Salt Lake City. In this post-war era of corruption, Huntington usually got his way.[7]

By early 1869, the California company had decided that Ogden, a town north of Salt Lake City, would make the best point of junction. Such positioning would give the Central Pacific the advantage in tapping the rich mining trade of Idaho. But the Union Pacific wanted to meet its rival farther west. Finally, after a comedy of parallel grading by the two companies, a settlement was reached. The two roads would meet at Promontory for the ceremonies of completing the road, but the eastern terminus of the Central Pacific would be Ogden. The financially hungry Union Pacific would be compensated generously for the track between the two places.

It is done! Andrew J. Russell's famous wet plate of "East and West Shaking Hands at the Joining of the Last Rail" at Promontory, Utah, May 10, 1869. — AMERICAN GEOGRAPHICAL SOCIETY

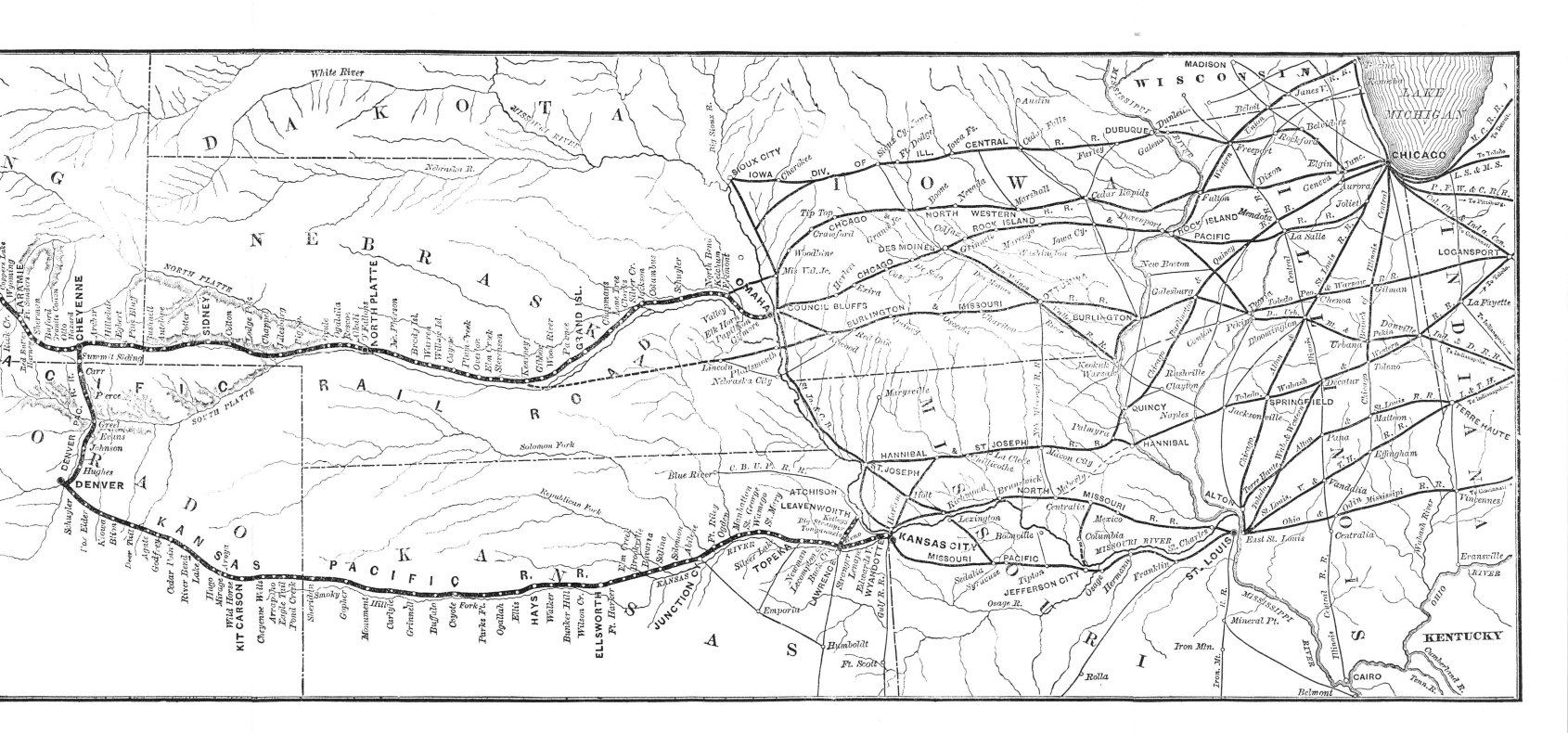

Before federal subsidies could be collected by the Central Pacific, government inspectors made an inspection of the completed work. Here commissioners, protected from the cold by buffalo robes, sit on the *Falcon's* pilot during such an inspection trip. — SOUTHERN PACIFIC COLLECTION

Desiring a more western junction, Chicagoans were infuriated when Congress ratified the agreement of the two companies. "For Congress to step in now and arbitrarily fix the point of junction at Ogden, when the Union Pacific has long since passed that point, is . . . rank injustice," stormed the *Chicago Tribune*. Chicago's loss was San Francisco's gain.[8]

With the completion of the "colossus of roads," as one contemporary wit called the Pacific railroad, celebrations occurred in every major American city. Throughout the nation, telegraphic wires were so connected that bells of every description would instantaneously send the message of the driving of the last spike. In San Francisco, the people turned out for military and civilian parades. In Chicago, Vice President Colfax reviewed massive demonstrations of excited humanity. Free trains carried crowds to California's capital to hear Governor Henry Haight commemorate the moment and extol the enterprise of Sacramento. After the initial telegraphic notice of the golden spike ceremony had ignited the celebrations, a simple message arrived at the Central Pacific's office in Sacramento: "Last spike driven. Leland Stanford." On May 10, 1869, the dream of a generation had become a reality.[9]

THE UNION
—AND—
CENTRAL PACIFIC R. R. LINE.

THE ONLY ALL RAIL ROUTE

Across the American Continent

AVOIDING DANGERS BY SEA.

This Route is Safest for Travelers,

MOST ATTRACTIVE FOR TOURISTS,

MOST DIRECT FOR EMIGRANTS,

TO THE GREAT AGRICULTURAL SECTIONS OF

NEBRASKA, COLORADO, WYOMING, UTAH AND IDAHO,

AND THE

RICH MINING DISTRICTS OF MONTANA, NEVADA AND CALIFORNIA.

By this Route the Traveler Witnesses the Beauties of the

GREAT VALLEY OF THE PLATTE

Which grows every kind of Crop by easy culture.

THE GREAT NATURAL PASTURES OF LARAMIE PLAINS,

Where Sheep and Cattle are fatted, and finest butter produced without the labor of feeding or housing stock.

THE GREAT IRON AND COAL FIELDS

Between Carbon and Evanston, over 300 miles in length.

MAGNIFICENT PANORAMA OF THE ROCKY MOUNTAINS.

At Sherman, **8,242** feet above the sea, the Line Passes the Highest Point in the World Crossed by Railroad. At Creston the Road passes the BACKBONE OF THE CONTINENT, where waters divide, flowing to the Atlantic and Pacific.

THE UNION PACIFIC RAILROAD

Passing between the great Natural Walls of Echo and Weber Canyons, connects at Union Junction with

THE CENTRAL PACIFIC RAILROAD

Which runs through the Mountain Passes and elevated Valleys of the Sierra Nevadas, and over the rich Plains of California to the Golden Gate.

THE UNION AND CENTRAL PACIFIC RAILROAD LINE

Is a wonderful achievement of Engineering skill and perfection in Railroad construction. The numerous connections by Rail, Steamers and Stages enable the Traveler to reach any point in

CALIFORNIA, OREGON, BRITISH AMERICA

OR ACROSS THE PACIFIC OCEAN TO

AUSTRALIA, NEW ZEALAND, HAWAII, JAPAN, CHINA AND INDIA.

Flags, crowds and bells witnessed for San Francisco the completion of the first transcontinental railroad. By 1869, San Franciscans saw the triumph of the once hated Central Pacific as in their interests. — SOUTHERN PACIFIC COLLECTION

"We will carry your freight from Sacramento to Ogden as cheap, mile for mile, as the Union Pacific Company will carry from Omaha," pledged an official of the Central Pacific soon after the cheering had stopped. The directors also promised that as soon as the railroad was completed to San Francisco, the merchants of that city would be charged no more for freight shipments to eastern cities than were their Sacramento counterparts. The company mistakenly believed these policies would satisfy their mercantile customers. "They ought not to be permitted to discriminate against Sacramento by charging as much from here to Omaha as from San Francisco, 130 miles farther," cried a Sacramento newspaper. Nevada towns also complained of the company's rate structure designed to encourage the long haul: "These rates are so adjusted

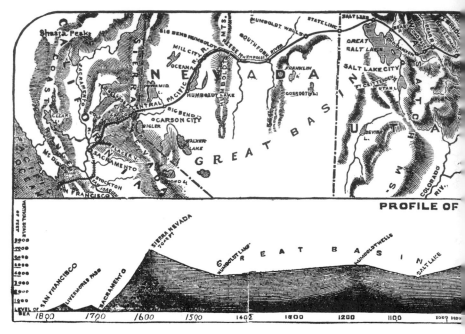

that it is cheaper to travel over the whole road than to travel over two-thirds of it." Years later, a Central Pacific freight agent in Nevada would recall that he had "nearly worn out perhaps the best pair of lungs that a man ever had in trying to justify that condition of things."[10]

Despite her newly-won commercial empire, San Francisco was also the scene of growing complaints against the Central Pacific. For several years, predictions had circulated that the completion of the Pacific railroad would multiply the riches of San Francisco's propertied class. European immigrants willing to work for low wages would supposedly rush to California on the cars of the Central Pacific. Wage costs would fall; and with the increase in population, property values would rise. But the rich did not become richer in 1869. The poor of the world, unable to pay the high fares, did not come West. Thus burst the bubble of San Francisco real estate prices that had grown from great expectations. Other factors as well contributed to San Francisco's growing disillusionment with the railroad. In the first several months of the line's operation, the Central Pacific's rate discrimination against eastern merchants was not enough to keep "the cheap John traffickers from Chicago" from

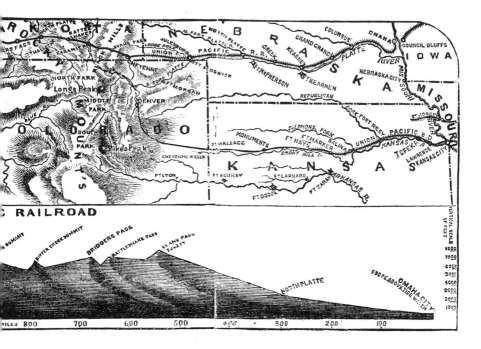

Profile of the completed Pacific Railroad. The railroad was built through harsh and lonely terrain, much of it mountainous. In the 1850's statesmen had argued whether or not the central route provided the most suitable path for a railroad. — HARPERS WEEKLY — 1869

invading San Francisco's commercial territory. Ultimately, the western company adjusted its rates to protect the commerce of California merchants from the "bagmen and drummers" of Chicago and St. Louis. However, in the meantime, many weaker San Francisco firms failed, adding to anti-railroad sentiment in the city.[11]

Although temporarily joyful over the completion of the transcontinental railroad, San Franciscans quickly became embittered that the Central Pacific had not fulfilled all of its supposed promises. Primary among these was the old dream that a transcontinental railroad would send the riches of the Orient pouring through San Francisco's portals. The opening of the Suez Canal six months after the completion of the Pacific railroad effectively ended this hope. Fifteen years in the making, the canal had received little attention in California throughout the 1860's. However, the realities of commerce could not be ignored in 1869 and 1870. The disappointment of many San Franciscans found an outlet in new anti-Central Pacific hostility, which would be released in the battles over the selection of the line's permanent terminus.[12]

NOTES

1. *Daily Alta California*, Aug. 7, 1862, 2:2-4; Daniel Boorstin, *The Americans, The National Experience* (New York, 1965), p. 256; Wesley Griswold, *A Work of Giants, Building the First Transcontinental Railroad* (New York, 1962), pp. 16-17, 50-51, 58.

2. *Chicago Tribune*, May 10, 1869 (found in Bancroft Scraps [Bancroft Library, University of California, Berkeley], LXXX, 1185); James McCague, *Moguls and Iron Men, The Story of the First Transcontinental Railroad* (New York, 1964), p. 64.

3. *Congressional Globe*, 38 Cong., 1 sess. (appendix), pp. 250-253; 39 Cong., 1 sess. (appendix), pp. 333-334; *Testimony Taken by the United States Pacific Railway Commission, Appointed Under the Act of Congress Approved March 3, 1887* (Washington, 1887), V, 2464, 2523; unidentified newspaper, July 2, 1864 (found in Bancroft Scraps, LXXX, 1076-1079).

4. *Daily Alta California*, Oct. 8, 1866, 2:1-2; *ibid.*, Aug. 19, 1868 (found in Bancroft Scraps, LXXX, 690); the concept of "urban imperialism" is borrowed from Richard C. Wade's *The Urban Frontier, The Rise of Western Cities, 1790-1830* (Cambridge, Mass., 1959), p. 336.

5. Collis P. Huntington, *Letters from Collis P. Huntington to Mark Hopkins, Leland Stanford, Charles Crocker, E. B. Crocker, Charles F. Crocker, and David D. Colton* (New York, 1892-1894), I, 5; James McCague, *Moguls and Iron Men*, pp. 156, 198.

6. *Quincy Union*, Nov. (day unknown), 1867 (found in Bancroft Scraps, LXXX, 74); Huntington, *Letters from Collis P. Huntington*, I, 193, 307; *Solano County Advertiser*, Feb. 13, 1869 (found in Bancroft Scraps, LXXX, 134-135); *Lassen Sage Brush*, Nov. 7, 1868 (found in Bancroft Scraps, LXXX, 1133); *Chico Courant*, Nov. 27, 1868 (found in Bancroft Scraps, LXXX, 925); *Marysville Appeal*, Dec. 13, 1868 (found in Bancroft Scraps, LXXX, 926).

7. Huntington, *Letters from Collis P. Huntington*, I, 205, 376; *Washington Evening Star*, April 3, 1869 (found in Bancroft Scraps, LXXX, 1170); McCague, *Moguls and Iron Men*, pp. 281-287.

8. *Sacramento Union*, Feb. 22, 1869 (found in Bancroft Scraps, LXXX, 712); *Cincinnati Gazette*, (month and day unknown), 1869 (found in Bancroft Scraps, LXXX, 987); Huntington, *Letters from Collis P. Huntington*, I, 418; Griswold, *A Work of Giants*, pp. 293-294; *Chicago Tribune*, April 3, 1869 (found in Bancroft Scraps, LXXX, 1167).

9. *New York Sun*, May 10, 1869 (found in Bancroft Scraps, LXXX, 1177); *Chicago Tribune*, May 11, 1869 (found in Bancroft Scraps, LXXX, 1189); Rockwell Hunt, *Golden Jubilee of the Pacific Railroad* (n.p., n.d.), pp. 7-8; Henry H. Haight, *Address Delivered at Sacramento, 1869, Upon the Completion of the Pacific Railroad* (San Francisco, 1869), p. 12; Stanford to Cen-

tral Pacific, May 10, 1869, Leland Stanford Correspondence (Stanford University Library, Stanford, California).

10. Unidentified newspaper, May 19, 1869 (found in Bancroft Scraps, LXXX, 1201); Huntington, *Letters from Collis P. Huntington*, I, 442; unidentified Sacramento newspaper, (month and day unknown), 1869 (found in Bancroft Scraps, XXXII, 5); unidentified Golden City newspaper, Aug. 22, 1869 (found in Bancroft Scraps, LXXX, 1228); *Testimony Taken by the U.S. Pacific Railway Commission*, VI, 3268; for examples of rate discrimination against Nevada towns see: Thomas H. Thompson and Albert A. West, *History of Nevada, 1881* (Berkeley, 1958: reprint of 1881 edition), p. 276; *San Francisco Bulletin*, Sept. 24, 1873, 2:2.

11. *Daily Alta California*, April 3, 1867 (found in Bancroft Scraps, LXXX, 1111); *ibid.*, Aug. 21, 1872, 2:1; *ibid.*, Sept. 4, 1872 (found in Bancroft Scraps, LXXX, 807); *San Francisco Bulletin*, Oct. (day unknown), 1868 (found in Bancroft Scraps, LXXX, 1129).

12. *Testimony Taken by the U.S. Pacific Railway Commission*, V, 2782; unidentified newspaper, July 20, 1869 (found in Bancroft Scraps, LXXX, 1317).

PART
THREE

The Octopus

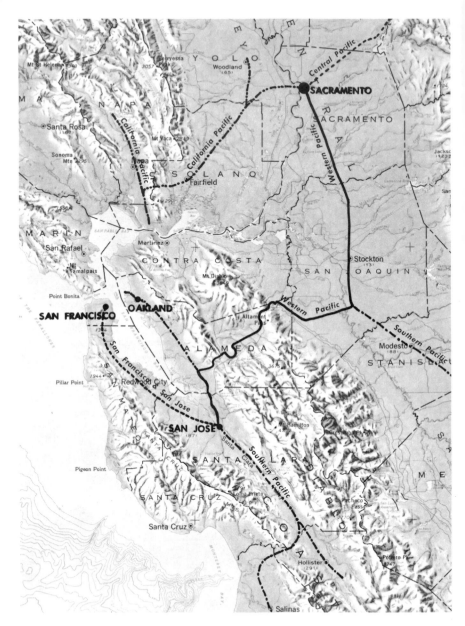

Competition between the California Pacific and the Western Pacific, both shown on the map above, increased the uncertainty regarding the permanent western terminus of the Pacific Railroad. Many San Francisco bay area communities joined the struggle for the prize.

7

Terminal Fever

THE completion of the Pacific railroad to Sacramento revived a question that had long concerned Californians. Which locality would supersede Sacramento as the final terminus? Leland Stanford and his associates had seemingly decided the matter in 1867 by their purchase of the Western Pacific, the line connecting the Central Pacific's Sacramento terminus with the San Francisco and San Jose Railroad's terminus at San Jose.[1] Rumors were then rife that the Central Pacific might soon buy the latter road as well, which would give the Central Pacific continuous track into San Francisco, making it the terminus of the transcontinental railroad. But the Western Pacific's new owners were not entirely content with the lengthy, roundabout, and costly route into the bay city via San Jose and soon let it be known that several sites other than San Francisco were under consideration for the permanent terminus.

Land speculators frantically bought lots in all potential locations: Oakland, Alameda, Goat (Yerba Buena) Island, South San Francisco, Vallejo, Ravenswood (now East Palo Alto), and Redwood City. "This mysterious terminus has caused almost as much excitement as the great Washoe mines created five and six years since," wrote one observer.[2] The Central Pacific's directors heightened the speculative character of terminus politics by letting it be known that the community granting them the most land and monetary subsidies would stand the best chance of winning. The enigmatic quality of the selection process was likewise enhanced, for not even the Central Pacific's leaders knew which community would be most generous with its resources. Nevertheless, they quite actively tried to determine the result. Company agents lobbied in Sacramento for terminal facilities along San Francisco's state-controlled waterfront. Even though the land desired was under water and would have to be developed by the company, the request was exorbitant — 8.5 miles of the city's waterfront, from Channel Street to Point San Bruno.

San Franciscans would have none of this scheme. Real estate owners in the principal part of the city, northwest of the proposed grant, saw possible ruin. "The proposition is essentially one for the founding of another city several miles south of the present location of San Francisco," cried the *Alta California*. "For where trade is, there population will move." Bay city residents saw the Central Pacific's request primarily as a land grab designed to create vast speculative profits, for the company was concurrently negotiating for control of Oakland's entire waterfront and lobbying in Congress for possession of the federally owned Goat Island, which today anchors the girders of the San Francisco-Oakland Bay Bridge. San Franciscans were pleased when the legislature released only 30 acres to the company along the city's northeastern shore. However, several days later, they were shocked as they learned that Oakland had given its entire waterfront to the Central Pacific. Nevertheless, San Francisco's cross-bay rival received no guarantees that it would be the permanent terminus, for the directors were waiting for more communities to offer their bounty.[3]

Meanwhile, state officials so laid out the 30 acres granted to the company that San Francisco was effectively removed from consideration as the terminus. First of all, the grant was divided into blocks dissected by city streets, disregarding the railroad's request that the land not be subdivided. More importantly, the survey required the company to keep its railroad tracks 300 feet from the waterfront. Such a situation would produce unnecessary delays and drayage costs in the handling of freight. At a time when the

Pacific railroad was competing with the Suez Canal for the trade of the Orient, these factors could not be tolerated.[4] Significantly, this development added to the attractiveness of Goat Island. The island had already been highly regarded by the company, for it could welcome the largest ocean-going vessels, which made it superior to Oakland's shallow port. Likewise, the island now appeared to possess advantages over San Francisco as well, for unlike the latter city's waterfront, Goat Island could be controlled entirely by the Central Pacific interests, once the federal government could be persuaded to give it up. Ultimately, the company intended to bridge the waters separating the island from Oakland, making Goat Island an extended Oakland port facility.

Many disparate interests opposed the company in its efforts to acquire the island. San Franciscans were especially hostile, fearing a rival city emerging in the middle of the bay. Although the island was small, shoals on its northern shore could be filled to increase its size, which was actually done generations later. Real estate speculators, owning land at rival terminal spots, jointly opposed the granting of the island. Even the company's Oakland allies dramatically joined the opposition by offering to buy the island from the United States for $1,000,000. They wanted the railroad company to pressure Congress to develop its harbor rather than divert trade to Goat Island. Rival railroad companies of all sizes had lobbyists fighting the Goat Island grant in Congress. The Union Pacific, the Northern Pacific, and the Atlantic and Pacific — all transcontinental lines with hopes of building to San Francisco Bay — would consent to a Goat Island bill only if they were guaranteed future facilities on the island. The California Pacific, a company building from Vallejo to Sacramento and Marysville, had similar desires. But this Huntington would not allow. Writing his companions from the East in 1868, he expressed his determination "to fight them all and get all or nothing." The island was not large enough to divide with potential competition.[5]

Military interests, claiming that Goat Island was necessary for the defense of the bay, also blocked the path of the Central Pacific. Despite the strong fortifications at several points around the bay, many citizens remembering the recent Civil War held that Goat Island should be reserved for long range guns. In fact, even before

A westbound double-headed freight train eases around Cape Horn, high above the abyss of the American River. With the completion of the transcontinental railroad, the question of where freight trains would terminate came to the fore. — DONALD DUKE COLLECTION

the terminus controversy, the *Alta California* called for the fortification of the island: "We take New Orleans and Mobile as examples. What happened to them may happen to us also. . . . We do not desire, in the event of war, to see hostile fleets run by Fort Point and Alcatraz, and our city placed at the mercy of their commanding officer." Army officers in San Francisco encouraged these fears, and Huntington was convinced that he knew the wellspring of their actions. Many of them owned fine cottages on the island that would have to come down if the company succeeded. General Henry W. Halleck of Civil War fame also feared the competition from a potential quarry on the island with his own rock supply business on Telegraph Hill in the city.[6]

These various opponents were strong enough to block passage of a Goat Island bill in the late 1860's. Because of this, Oakland's civic leaders optimistically believed that their community would be the permanent terminus. Upon the Central Pacific's arrival in Oakland in the fall of 1869, massive demonstrations and long speeches proclaimed Oakland's future as "the railroad center of the State." Federal improvement of Oakland's harbor would insure this result. But in the eyes of Oakland's commercial propagandists, dredging the harbor would be merely a small amendment to God's already existing accomplishment, for Nature had "ordained Oakland as the great terminus of the railroad system of the Pacific Coast."[7]

"If the Pacific Railroad Company can build up Oakland into the chief city of California, it will be done," noted a Vallejo newspaper, "but Vallejo stands in the way." This claim was more then the usual airy boasting, for the Central Pacific system's principal rival in the State, the California Pacific, terminated in Vallejo. The California Pacific was completed to Sacramento in February 1869 and shortly thereafter to Marysville. Talk was then plentiful that the Union Pacific would build into California through Beckwourth's Pass, making connection with the California Pacific. With such a prospect before them, the citizens of Vallejo were eager for combat with Oakland. And like the partisans of the latter city, they claimed the blessing of Providence:

> The mistake of attempting to build up a terminus at Oakland would be greater than that of crossing the Sierra by the Truckee route, and everybody will see it in a few years. That which is

The California Pacific was the first serious California rival to the Central Pacific. With the most direct line from Sacramento to San Francisco Bay, the California Pacific indeed threatened the burgeoning monopoly of the Big Four. In the view above, California Pacific *Vallejo* No. 5 at the head of the Knight's Landing train at Woodland in 1871. (BELOW) *D. C. Haskins* No. 11, near Hornbrook, during the construction of the Oregon & California. — BOTH GERALD M. BEST COLLECTION

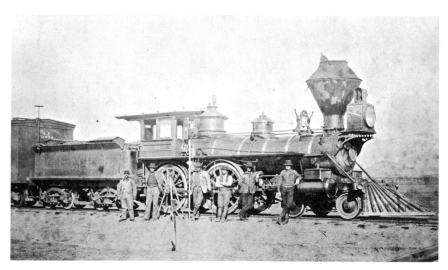

cheapest and best for the public is most profitable for the company. It will not pay to buck against nature. The mountains and the sea are not to be fooled with. Beckwourth's Pass is the natural entrance to the State for the cars, and Vallejo for the ships.

The California Pacific possessed definite competitive advantages over its rival. Its rail line from Sacramento to tidewater was 50 miles shorter than the Central Pacific's connection with San Francisco Bay. It was also favored with an easier grade than its competitor, which had to climb the relatively steep Livermore Pass between Oakland and Stockton. In fact, transcontinental passengers from the East, bound for San Francisco, often surrendered their tickets at Sacramento and took the speedier route by way of Vallejo, where swift steamers would shuttle them to San Francisco. Disillusioned after a year of competition, Huntington wrote: "One more road like the W.P. [Western Pacific] would break us."[8]

The California Pacific pressed its opponent without relief. In 1868, the Central Pacific had purchased the California and Oregon Railroad, a company guaranteed federal aid from Marysville to the southern boundary of Oregon. Late in the following year, the California Pacific announced plans to build up the Sacramento Valley to Shasta. This threat to parallel the California and Oregon line was a transparent attempt to injure their rival's enterprise in the money markets of the world. Yet the Central Pacific's directors maintained a poker-faced calm and continued to slash rates between Sacramento and Oakland. However, their poise was shattered in mid-1871, when the California Pacific stated that if the Union Pacific would not build to it, it would build through Beckwourth's Pass, thus creating a second western branch of the transcontinental railroad. The resulting anxiety in Central Pacific circles was best explained years later by John Putnam Jackson, President of the California Pacific in 1871:

> The Central Pacific Railroad was built under such circumstances of pressure as to time and difficulty of realizing on its securities and the great cost of material at that time, being shortly after war, that the new road projected by the California Pacific could have been built at a very much less cost, to wit, one-half, and would not have been burdened when finished with the indebtedness that handicapped the Central Pacific. I may say that it was a constant threat that some other company would parallel the

97

The terminus-wharf of the Central Pacific, was photographed from Goat Island in the 1870's. This structure running from the Oakland shore line some 11,000 feet, contained a passenger depot, railroad offices, warehouses and storage facilities. — WRIGHTWOOD COLLECTION

Central Pacific, which the Central Pacific had to guard against by every means in its power.[9]

In order to maintain the financial position of the Central Pacific, Huntington and his associates bought the California Pacific in the summer of 1871. Because the Central Pacific was concurrently purchasing other potential competing lines and buying stock back from counties threatening stockholders' suits, it unhappily found itself in financial straits. Ironically, in order to prevent the Central Pacific's bankruptcy by cutthroat competition, the company's directors had driven it further into debt. And in the course of creating a monopolistic position in the State, most of the company's directors had exhausted themselves and began thinking of early retirement. Charles Crocker actually sold out to his partners several months before the California Pacific purchase.[10]

Although disappointed by the sale of the California Pacific, Vallejo's citizens did not despair. Watching the directors build major terminal facilities at Oakland, Vallejans believed that the company would retain their port as a major grain shipping facility. Sadly, their dream never materialized, for after 1871 heavy rains brought frequent flooding along the California Pacific's track. Because of this inconvenience, the California Pacific's original route was abandoned. In 1879, the company opened a new short line on higher ground, from Oakland to Sacramento via Martinez and Benicia, several miles southeast of Vallejo, which was "left to stagnation."[11]

While the public focused on the dramatic Central Pacific/California Pacific competition, work quietly progressed along Oakland's waterfront. Because of the lack of deep-water port facilities there, the directors built a wharf 11,000 feet long running from the Oakland shore line out to a depth of 24 feet at low tide. The huge structure, complete with passenger depot, railroad offices, warehouses, and outside storage facilities, gradually became part of San Francisco's view of the bay. When construction was completed in January 1871, San Franciscans became fully aware of the commercial threat of the new wharf. Most overland rail commerce and most of the shipping business of California could now by-pass the wharves of their city. To climax San Francisco's frus-

99

With Goat Island casting a shadow in the background, a local passenger train has just pulled in to the wharf depot and unloaded its passengers who will take the ferry on to San Francisco. Being of wood piling construction, the wharf was vulnerable to wood-eating mollusks. — GERALD M. BEST COLLECTION

tration, the California Pacific's offices were moved from San Francisco to Sacramento in 1871. Fears began to grow that San Francisco's eminence lay in the past, as her real estate values relative to other towns continued to drop.[12]

Railroad officials slowly discovered, however, that their Oakland pier was endangered. The rapid flow of the tides around the end of the pier, where large warehouses were located, was washing away the mud bottom, weakening the foundation of the whole structure. Thousands of tons of rubble were dumped into the bay at this spot, but the natural scouring of the relentless tides defeated all efforts. The ravenous teredo, a wood-eating mollusk, likewise

threatened to undermine the wooden structure. With reserved satisfaction, the *Alta California* described the effects of these occurrences on Oakland's commerce:

> Under these two destructive influences, a southeaster, such as we
> sometimes have in the winter months, may in a night annihilate
> that costly depot, and with it sweep into the bay the thousands
> of tons of wheat and other merchandise piled up waiting ship-
> ment. These dangers are of so important a character that insur-
> ance is difficult to effect, except at high rates, upon merchandise
> stored at that point.[13]

Fearing a disaster on the pier, the company reactivated its
efforts to acquire Goat Island, which could serve as a thoroughly
safe location for depots and warehouses. When the directors purchased 150 acres on shoal lands just north and adjoining the island, the old spector of a rival city arose. A Committee of One
Hundred, composed of San Francisco merchants opposing the
Goat Island scheme, marshalled arguments against the grant and
sent lobbyists to Washington. The angry merchants claimed that
the company's plan to build a rock bridge from Oakland to the
island would alter tidal movements in the bay and increase the
current's velocity along San Francisco's waterfront, thus endanger-
ing the city's commerce. Military authorities again asserted that
the island was necessary for the defense of the harbor, despite
General William T. Sherman's admission that fortifying Goat Island "would be about as wise as for a man to plant a cannon on
the steps of his house to protect it."[14] Huntington also had his lobbyists in Congress. They argued that the regulation forbidding ship
and rail car to come together on San Francisco's waterfront necessitated locating the terminus of the Pacific railroad elsewhere.
Furthermore, the Central Pacific pointed out, farmers desired to
ship their wheat from a port free from the tolls collected on San
Francisco's state-controlled shoreline. In short, acquisition of Goat
Island would prevent "the rapacious clique" of dishonest state ad-
ministrators, San Francisco warehouse owners, and city draymen
from robbing the shippers of the state. The island was needed for
the commerce of state and nation.[15]

While this fight raged on, the Committee of One Hundred
investigated opportunities for luring projected transcontinental

railroads into San Francisco. The possibility of a southern transcontinental line terminating in the city was especially attractive. A southern road, built over level terrain, could offer lower rates than the only existing line, while avoiding the snows that periodically obstructed the Central Pacific; and San Francisco would no longer have to fear for her commercial future. Optimistically, the Committee began communicating with the Atlantic and Pacific Railroad Company,* a firm possessing a Congressional subsidy to build a transcontinental line into California along the 35th parallel.[16]

The rising expectations of the Committee of One Hundred in 1872 were balanced by the growing pessimism of Collis Huntington. With the Goat Island battle, with increasing financial problems created by buying out rivals, and with the thought of his company's monopoly ending with the construction of the Atlantic and Pacific into San Francisco, Huntington's soul demanded freedom from the burdens of his office. "I am losing my grip," he wrote to his California colleagues. President Grant, fearing for California's Republican Party in an election year, wanted him to drop his efforts on Goat Island until the following year. Everything seemed to be going wrong for the beleaguered railroad magnate.[17]

Meanwhile, a quarrel was brewing between the recently courted Atlantic and Pacific company and San Francisco's merchants. The San Franciscans desired to control the western end of the Atlantic and Pacific to insure that the company's rate schedules would discriminate in favor of their city's commerce. The Atlantic and Pacific, an institution based in St. Louis, refused, causing the editor of the *Alta California* to roar in anger: "Shall San Francisco stand erect among the great commercial centers of our country, controlling her own destinies, or shall she become a suburb of St. Louis and Chicago, and the thrall of New York? That is the issue which is before our people today." Seeing his opposition divided and confused, Huntington made his move. He and Hopkins announced they were willing to sell their interests in the Southern Pacific, a recently purchased projected southern transcontinental road with

---

*The Atlantic and Pacific should not be confused with the Pacific and Atlantic, which was the precursor of the San Francisco and San Jose Railroad.

a Congressional subsidy, to interested San Franciscans. When built, this line could connect with the Atlantic and Pacific, or with the Texas and Pacific, a projected 32nd parallel transcontinental railroad. And San Francisco would continue to dominate the commerce of the West. Shortly thereafter, Huntington also began discussing the possibilities of selling the Central Pacific to San Franciscans.[18]

A minority of the Committee of One Hundred, remaining loyal to the Atlantic and Pacific, ignored Huntington's offer and set out to get a proposition placed before San Franciscans in the November elections to subsidize their company with $10,000,000. But most of the Committee refused to be dragged along by "the train of St. Louis." They formed a sham corporation, named the San Francisco and Colorado Railroad, and like their rival asked for $10,000,000 from the city, it being common knowledge that this money would be used toward the purchase of the Southern Pacific. Most of these merchants also sought better relations with the Central Pacific through a compromise which was reached in August of 1872. By the settlement, the company would permanently stop its efforts to acquire Goat Island and would build a bridge at Ravenswood (East Palo Alto). Then its track could come into San Francisco as easily as Oakland. The main traffic of the company would then be transferred to the new San Francisco route. For its part, the city would vote a $2,500,000 subsidy for the bridge and would use its influence to allow track up to and on the city's wharves. In a close vote, the Committee of One Hundred consented to the Ravenswood compromise and then adjourned *sine die*.[19]

Events had moved quickly to resolve old conflicts. But before any of these subsidy schemes could appear on the November ballot, San Francisco's Board of Supervisors and Mayor had to give their assent. The Supervisors overwhelmingly opposed the Atlantic and Pacific and strongly favored the rival subsidy that would purchase the Southern Pacific. But the directors of the latter project, after informally canvassing the city and finding strong anti-subsidy feeling, decided to withdraw voluntarily from the contest. A state-wide weariness of voting gifts to companies which later reneged on supposed promises, coupled with the Crédit Mobilier scandal on the national scene, accounted for this opposition. Even the Ravenswood compromise died when the Supervisors amended and strengthened the provision that the company would *permanently* divert most of its business into San Francisco. Leland Stanford refused to consent to this change, for he planned to shift the bulk of his traffic again back to Oakland following the construction of a new efficient line from Oakland to Sacramento via Martinez and Benicia. With this dispute, the original compromise failed to be placed before the voters, although over a majority of them had signed a petition favoring the agreement.[20]

The struggles of 1872 had solved none of the problems tiring both the Central Pacific's managers and the citizens of San Francisco. Ultimately, however, the drift of events restored reasonably good feelings between the two. Hopkins and the exhausted Huntington never did sell out, although the latter's correspondence for the next several years was peppered with expressions of a desire to do so. The financial panic of 1873 wiped away all potential offers to buy and in fact propelled Charles Crocker back into the company from which he was unable to collect his due. The unfolding exposé of the Crédit Mobilier helped strangle all new governmental largess to railroad companies for the rest of the decade, causing the Goat Island "grab," as opponents of the Central Pacific called it, to be forgotten early the next year. Afterwards, the company divided its terminal business between several localities. Although San Francisco never became the company's principal point of transshipment, it did achieve the honor of becoming the home office of all holdings of the Central Pacific in September 1873. To San Franciscans, the transfer of the headquarters of these firms was symbolically important. A rumor in 1873 that Huntington had declined to sell the Southern Pacific to eastern interests unconcerned with "the material interests of any particular locality" also helped San Franciscans to appreciate how much the directors were allied to the commerce of San Francisco.[21] For most of the remainder of the decade, merchants of the city, while not totally happy with the railroad monopoly, would recognize that it did indeed discriminate in their favor and against men of commerce in rival communities.

NOTES

1. Stanford to Hopkins, Feb. 5, 1867, Leland Stanford Correspondence (Stanford University Library, Stanford, California); Hopkins to Huntington, April 10, 1867, Huntington MSS (microfilm, Huntington Library, San Marino, Calif.).
2. *Daily Alta California*, April 13, 1868 (found in Bancroft Scraps [Bancroft Library, University of California, Berkeley], LXXX, 1309).
3. *Ibid.*, Mar. 9, 1868 (found in Bancroft Scraps, LXXX, 1118-1119); *ibid.*, April 3, 1868 (found in Bancroft Scraps, LXXX, 1120); *San Francisco Bulletin*, Mar. 28, 1868, 2:1.
4. George Clark, *Leland Stanford, War Governor of California, Railroad Builder and Founder of Stanford University* (Stanford, 1931), pp. 316-317; *Daily Alta California*, Jan. 9, 1873 (found in Bancroft Scraps, LXXX, 812).
5. Collis P. Huntington, *Letters from Collis P. Huntington to Mark Hopkins, Leland Stanford, Charles Crocker, E. B. Crocker, Charles F. Crocker, and David D. Colton* (New York, 1892-1894), I, 14, 62, 211, 267, 365; *ibid.*, II 203, 314; *Testimony Taken by the United States Pacific Railway Commission, Appointed Under the Act of Congress Approved March 3, 1887* (Washington, 1887), VI, 3170-3171; *Daily Alta California*, Mar. 9, 1872 (found in Bancroft Scraps, LXXX, 771); *ibid.*, Feb. 10, 1868 (found in Bancroft Scraps, LXXX, 681).
6. Huntington, *Letters from Collis P. Huntington*, I, 200-201, 273; *Daily Alta Cailfornia*, Oct. 21, 1866, 2:1.
7. Central Pacific Railroad Co. (John Scott), *Information Concerning the Terminus of the Railroad System of the Pacific Coast* (Oakland, 1871), p. 25; *Daily Alta California*, Nov. 9, 1869 (found in Bancroft Scraps, LXXX, 1232-1233).
8. *Solano County Advertiser*, Feb. 13, 1869 (found in Bancroft Scraps, LXXX, 1154); *ibid.*, Mar. 13, 1869 (found in Bancroft Scraps, LXXX, 713-714); *Daily Alta California*, Feb. 5, 1865, 1:5; Peter J. Delay, *History of Yuba and Sutter Counties, California* (Los Angeles, 1924), pp. 85-86; *Testimony Taken by the United States Pacific Railway Commission*, VI, 3613; Huntington, *Letters from Collis P. Huntington*, II, 53.
9. *Chico Courant*, Sept. 26, 1886 (found in Bancroft Scraps, LXXX, 121); *Butte Record*, Oct. 16, 1869 (found in Bancroft Scraps, LXXX, 153); *Daily Alta California*, May 19, 1871 (found in Bancroft Scraps, LXXX, 1247-1248); *Testimony Taken by the United States Pacific Railway Commission*, VI, 3629.
10. Julius Grodinsky, *Transcontinental Railway Strategy, 1869-1893: A Study of Businessmen* (Philadelphia, 1962), p. 27; Hubert H. Bancroft, *History of California* (San Francisco, 1890), VII, 586-588; Theodore Hittell, *History of California* (San Francisco, 1897), IV, 483-484; Huntington, *Letters from Collis P. Huntington*, II, 275.
11. Huntington, *Letters from Collis P. Huntington*, III, 159 c-d; *Letters from Mark Hopkins, Leland Stanford, Charles Crocker, Charles F. Crocker, and David D. Colton, to Collis P. Huntington. From Aug. 27, 1869 to Dec. 30, 1879* (New York, 1891), p. 192; Bancroft, *History of California*, VII, 685-686; *San Francisco Bulletin*, Nov. 28, 1879 (found in Bancroft Scraps, LXXX, 896).
12. Stuart Daggett, *Chapters on the History of the Southern Pacific* (Berkeley, 1922), p. 111; *Daily Alta California*, Jan. 15, 1871 (found in Bancroft Scraps, LXXX, 1245).
13. *Daily Alta California*, Jan. 9, 1873 (found in Bancroft Scraps, LXXX, 812).

14. *Ibid.*, Mar. 18, 1872 (found in Bancroft Scraps, LXXX, 772); *ibid.*, Jan. 5, 1873 (found in Bancroft Scraps, LXXX, 811); *ibid.*, Jan. 12, 1873, 2:1-2; *San Francisco Bulletin*, Nov. 28, 1873, 2:1-2; *Testimony Taken by the United States Pacific Railway Commission*, VI, 3170-3171.
15. *San Francisco Bulletin*, Sept. 30, 1873, 2:2; *San Diego Union*, Mar. 29, 1872 (found in Bancroft Scraps, LXXX, 422).
16. *San Francisco Bulletin*, Mar. 26, 1874, 2:2; *San Francisco Chronicle*, Feb. (day unknown), 1872 (found in Bancroft Scraps, LXXX, 961).
17. Huntington, *Letters from Collis P. Huntington*, II, 335-336.
18. *Daily Alta California*, May 4, 1872 (found in Bancroft Scraps, LXXX, 429); *ibid.*, Sept. 19, 1872 (found in Bancroft Scraps, LXXX, 189-187); *ibid.*, July 6, 1872, 1:5; Huntington, *Letters from Collis P. Huntington*, II, 393-394.
19. Huntington, *Letters from Collis P. Huntington*, II, 358-459; Bancroft, *History of California*, VII, 610; *Daily Alta California*, Aug. 17, 1872 (found in Bancroft Scraps, LXXX, 796); *ibid.*, Aug. 29, 1872, 1:3.
20. Robert E. Riegel, *The Story of Western Railroads, From 1852 Through the Reign of the Giants* (New York, 1926), pp. 78-79; Clark, *Leland Stanford*, pp. 320-321; *Daily Alta California*, Jan. 3, 1873, 1:1; Sept. 17, 1872, 1:2-3; Oct. 18, 1872, 2:2.
21. Huntington, *Letters from Collis P. Huntington*, III, 52; *San Francisco Bulletin*, Feb. 8, 1876 (found in Bancroft Scraps, LXXX, 567); *Daily Alta California*, April 1, 1873, 2:2; *ibid.*, Feb. 2, 1873 (found in Bancroft Scraps, LXXX, 813); *ibid.*, Oct. 10, 1873 (found in Bancroft Scraps, LXXX, 1265; Cornelius Cole, *Memoirs of Cornelius Cole, Ex-Senator of the United States From California* (New York, 1908), pp. 267-268; *Testimony Taken by the United States Pacific Railway Commission*, VI, 3162.

8

The Southern Pacific

THE planning of a southern transcontinental railroad began even before the completion of the Central Pacific. Shortly after the Civil War, businessmen realized that the first railroad across the continent would not satisfy even their own generation's needs, for it was closed periodically by a capricious "Mother Nature." The war, more than the requirements of trade, had led to the selection of the hazardous central route. With the coming of peace, the advantages of a southern line again received attention. With talk of a southern Pacific railroad in the air, the directors of the Central Pacific strove to minimize the weaknesses of their road. In the spring and summer of 1868, they built sturdy snow sheds over sections of the high Sierra track. But winter's ravages closed the route anyway, for the track of the Union Pacific was left largely unprotected by sheds due to the scarcity of timber on the plains and the unpredictability of drifts along its part of the line. Likewise, little could be done to ease the mountainous grades which made transportation expensive over the central route. Clearly only the construction of a new railroad bypassing these obstacles would suffice.[1]

In the early 1870's, it was popularly believed that a southern transcontinental line would capture the trade of the Orient, something that the central road had failed to do. And there would be other benefits. General Sherman testified that a railroad through Arizona would save the federal government $5,000,000 annually in transporting troops and supplies to fight the Apache menace. Governor J. W. Throckmorton of Texas astutely noted that it would also be a most effective way of bridging the "bloody chasm" wrought by the Civil War. Hence, pressures from various sources contributed to the post-war push for a southern Pacific railroad.[2]

Shortly after the war, Congress passed a bill subsidizing several companies to build the much-heralded southern road. In July 1866, a land grant equalling the terms of the Pacific Railroad Act of 1864 was bestowed upon both the Southern Pacific Railroad Company, then controlled by San Franciscans, and the Atlantic and Pacific Railroad Company, which was based in St. Louis. Although not endowed with federal *financial* assistance, these two firms were expected to rapidly construct their line, which would presumably meet at the Colorado River near the 35th parallel. Terminating in San Francisco via the San Francisco and San Jose Railroad, the Southern Pacific was enthusiastically supported by that city's commercial interests, as noted in the following *Alta California* editorial of 1868:

> The Central [Pacific] has its California terminus at Sacramento, 90 miles from San Francisco by the nearest route of travel, and 130 miles off by any practicable railroad route. The Western [Pacific] Company has accepted land for a terminus at Oakland, and is soliciting a grant of Goat Island from Congress. . . . The Central and Western Companies are not controlled by San Franciscans, and seem disposed to make their termini east of the Bay; the Directors of the Southern Pacific are San Francisco men, and and the natural terminus of the road would be in this city, even if the interests of the stockholders and Directors were not here.[3]

Unlike the Central Pacific's lines, the Southern Pacific needed no expensive detours to connect with San Francisco, for its route extended southward, down the peninsula along the coast. The Big Four, as the directors of the Central Pacific were coming to be called, were fully aware of the threat posed by the Southern Pacific. "I am inclined to think that it will be the road that will do most of the through business between New York and San Francisco," wrote Huntington of the Southern Pacific in 1868. "We cannot well overestimate this southern connection." Shortly thereafter, the Big Four purchased the Southern Pacific and its tracks into San Francisco. But several years would pass before the rumored purchase would be proven fact.

For over a decade, fear of potential southern transcontinental competition would shape much of the activity of the Central Pacific's directors. Stopping the threat of one possible rival was not enough. In order to prevent bankruptcy of their corporation, the Big Four had to overcome every competitive challenge, especially those in southern latitudes. In addition to the Southern Pacific, a similar threat arose in the San Joaquin Valley, where the Stockton and Tulare Railroad Company planned to link Stockton with Visalia, in opposition to the Central Pacific which announced its intention of building down the valley in 1868. The Stockton City Council, beseiged by both companies for public assistance, held hearings to ascertain which of the two firms would most benefit Stockton. Leland Stanford was a key witness. Council members, troubled by rumors that the Big Four's San Joaquin Valley extension would connect with the Central Pacific 12 miles south of Stockton, wanted assurances that theirs would be the junction city. Likewise, they demanded Stanford's guarantee that the aided company's rate structure would discriminate in favor of their community for the trade of the valley. Reportedly, Stanford was irritated by these questions, and when Stockton's mayor inquired, "Governor, what do you intend to charge for freight and passenger fares?" Stanford replied, "None of your damn business!" and left the room.[4]

Thus pitted against the Big Four, the city of Stockton could only support the Stockton and Tulare Company. But before it could subsidize the firm, the company sold out to Stanford. Stanford then created Lathrop, 12 miles south of Stockton, as a junction town for his east-west roads and his soon-to-be constructed San Joaquin valley extension. As construction crews began laying track down the valley, Stockton was left to reflect upon its lost opportunity. Undaunted, Stockton's leading citizens created a new south-bound rival to Stanford's interests in 1869 called the Stockton and Visalia Railroad. The following year, the community do-

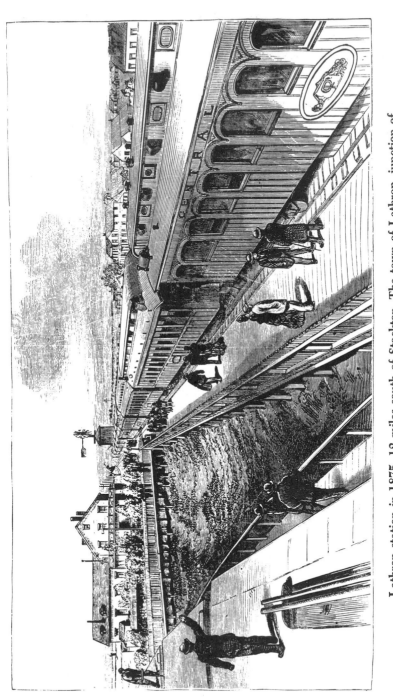

Lathrop station in 1875, 12 miles south of Stockton. The town of Lathrop, junction of the Central Pacific and Southern Pacific, was named after the maiden name of Leland Stanford's wife. Here passengers changed trains for the run down the San Joaquin Valley. — WRIGHTWOOD COLLECTION

Stocktonians were slow to forgive the railroad monopoly for creating Lathrop as the junction town, a role they had seen for their own city. Vainly placing their hopes in rival lines down the San Joaquin Valley, Stockton's citizens were to complain of the Big Four's high valley freight rates until the 1890's, when they gained temporary relief by the San Francisco & San Joaquin Valley Railway. In the scene above, a Central Pacific passenger train takes on water at the Stockton tank. (BELOW) The Stockton freight yard. — BOTH DONALD DUKE COLLECTION

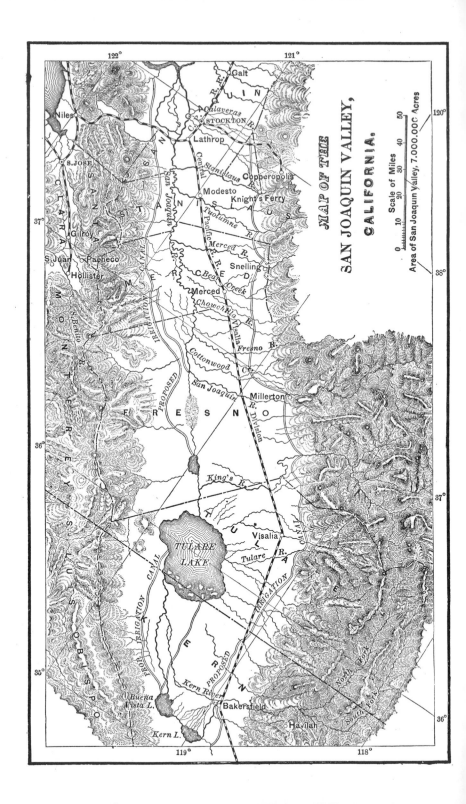

MAP OF THE

SAN JOAQUIN VALLEY,

CALIFORNIA.

Scale of Miles

0   10   20   30   40   50

Area of San Joaquin Valley, 7,000,000 Acres

nated large sums to this temporary champion of Stockton's local needs, but in 1871 this company too was purchased by the Big Four. Stockton's series of defeats left her citizens so deeply embittered against the Central Pacific that half a century later this attitude was still alive.[5]

The Central Pacific had acquired both the coastal and San Joaquin Valley connections of a southern transcontinental road, but the Big Four could not relax and enjoy their recent victories. To maintain their monopoly, they were forced to confront the most serious threat of transcontinental competition up to that date, this time emanating from San Diego. In the late 1860's, San Diego's railroad hopes had rested on John Charles Frémont, President of the Memphis, El Paso and Pacific Railroad Company. This firm had planned to terminate its line in San Diego, but in 1870 the company failed. Rebounding from this disappointment, San Diegans sought new transcontinental allies. They petitioned the Atlantic and Pacific to survey its line to San Diego, but this 35th-parallel road was then more interested in terminating in San Francisco. The Texas Pacific Railway Company, given a land grant by Congres in 1871 to build along the 32nd parallel, was a better prospect for San Diego, and a formal alliance was created between them in 1872. Arriving in San Diego late in August 1872, Tom Scott, President of the Texas Pacific, got down to the business of negotiating the contract that would bring his track from Texas to San Diego. Rich in vacant lots and poor in capital resources, the town's citizens granted 9,000 acres to Scott's company for terminal facilities. Diplomatically, he did not ask for a monetary subsidy and thus cemented a strong friendship with that community.[6]

Faced with the specter of a transcontinental competitor bound for San Diego, the Big Four made plans to build through the southern part of the State on the way to the Colorado River. Their goal was to occupy the best southern California route before Scott could reach the state line. Extremely pressed for funds because of their recent purchases, they saw an opportunity to squeeze a subsidy out of Los Angeles, whose townsmen feared being left off the main line of a southern transcontinental road. So the city's leaders and the Southern Pacific negotiated an agreement to be ratified by the town's voters in November 1872. The company committed it-

As the side-wheel towboat *Los Angeles* leaves the Wilmington wharf, a Los Angeles & San Pedro Railroad mixed train leaves for Los Angeles. In 1870, Los Angeles' only railroad was the Los Angeles & San Pedro Railroad, a short line built by Phineas Banning to provide a port connection. — DONALD DUKE COLLECTION

A birds eye view of Los Angeles in 1877. Held in disdain by its southern rival San Diego, Los Angeles recognized its potential and actively worked to lure the Southern Pacific to its gates. — WRIGHTWOOD COLLECTION

self to placing Los Angeles on its main line in exchange for a substantial monetary subsidy and control of a local railroad connecting Los Angeles with its port at Wilmington.[7]

Fearful of a firm alliance between the Southern Pacific and Los Angeles, Scott and San Diego made a rival offer. For the same monetary subsidy requested by the Southern Pacific, Scott and San Diego interests would build a railroad connecting Los Angeles and the Texas Pacific's terminus at San Diego. Raising the ante, the Southern Pacific promised that if its subsidy passed it would build a railroad from Los Angeles south to Anaheim. However, even before that, it was unlikely that Angelinos would vote for the San Diego subsidy, for both Los Angeles and San Diego had aspirations of becoming the chief city of southern California. The former had the advantage of greater population and richer surrounding countryside, while San Diego commanded the finest natural port in the southern part of the State. Angelinos were quick to note "that a city cannot be built and sustained without a productive [surrounding] country to support it, and that a harbor is of no avail to support a city without other aid." San Diegans replied that a metropolis could never rise near "the Wilmington slough, whose bottom lies too near the top." The alternative of voting for the San Diego connection, warned the *San Diego World,* was reduction of Los Angeles "into a slavish allegiance to San Francisco."[8] Los Angeles's choices were clear. Angelinos could establish their community as a way station on a road terminating in San Francisco or as a branch connection with a road terminating in San Diego. In November,

115

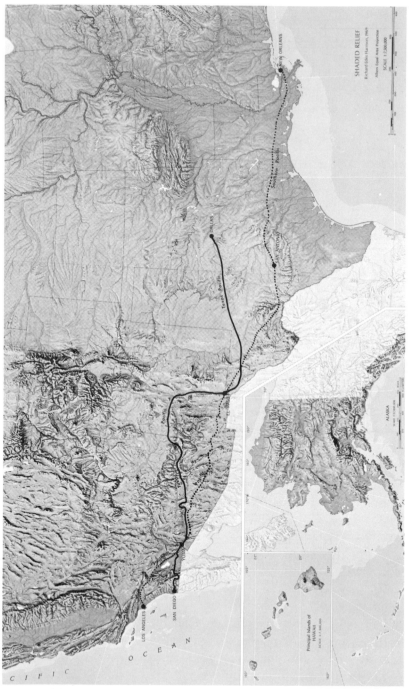

The projected route of the Texas Pacific roughly paralleled that of the Southern Pacific, which ultimately defeated the former company in the race to control the first southern transcontinental rail line.

they cast their ballots for the Southern Pacific. Hurt and angered by the decision of her northern neighbor, San Diego reacted haughtily, as reflected in a *San Diego World* editorial: "Los Angeles will shortly awaken from her dream of jealousy and discover that she will have to play 'back country' to San Diego anyhow. Her fruitful soil was compounded, and her pretty valleys hollowed out, especially that she might be one of those numerous auxiliaries which will build up the commerce of San Diego."[9]

San Diego still had the Texas Pacific, although its confidence in this line was somewhat shaken in the following year when Tom Scott announced his route into California. San Diegans had hoped Scott would build on a straight line from Ft. Yuma on the Colorado River to their town, but his chosen route swung northward from Ft. Yuma through the San Gorgonio Pass, from there proceeding southwestward to the coast and down to San Diego. Fears mounted in Scott's announced terminal town. Might not this roundabout route indicate that the real intentions of the Texas Pacific were to build northward to San Francisco, providing San Diego with only a branch road? Scott and his agents discounted such talk. The straight line would serve only shifting sand dunes, while the route selected would provide San Diego with her cherished "back country." With a style of humor appreciated in San Diego, one Texas Pacific executive told the worried citizenry that his company might "run a *branch* up to San Francisco, to enable San Franciscans to buy cheap goods in San Diego," but that was all. For the moment, San Diegans trusted the chosen instrument of their community's urban imperialism and dreamed of the time when their city would be "the purchasing mart for the whole State of California." Looking forward to that day, one San Diego propagandist announced: "our 'back country' will thus not only include southern Nevada, southern Utah, Arizona, southern California, New Mexico and the whole of northern Mexico, but will stretch to the very gates of the city of the Golden Gate."[10]

Of course, the dreams of San Diegans could only come true if the Texas Pacific built into California, an event Huntington and his friends were laboring hard to prevent. These opponents of San Diego were faced with a difficult problem. Much of the Southern Pacific's route traversed rugged terrain and would be most expensive to construct. On the other hand, the alternative survey down the San Joaquin Valley would cut through a level area of potentially rich farm lands, a region through which track could be quickly laid on the way to the Colorado River. However, this new San Joaquin Valley route of the Southern Pacific would receive no land grant, unless the federal government could be persuaded to approve the change. This was a most difficult proposition, because following the Crédit Mobilier scandal Congress was in an anti-subsidy mood, extremely reluctant to grant railroad corporations that which they desired. Nevertheless, assuming that the government would eventually assent to the change, the Big Four decided to build their southern transcontinental line down the San Joaquin Valley. Because of the uncertainty of what Congress would ultimately do, land titles in the valley remained vague for several years, causing settlers in parts of Tulare and Fresno Counties the frustration of not knowing if their land was really owned by the railroad. To the rue of these farmers, the Big Four were ultimately given title to the disputed land, a situation which would help bring about the Mussel Slough massacre of 1880. But long before the settlement of this dispute, the Big Four hurried construction down the valley toward Los Angeles. Simultaneously, the company's extension southeast of Los Angeles was surveyed through the San Gorgonio Pass toward Arizona, all of this energy being expended for the sole purpose of beating Scott.[11]

The war between the Texas Pacific and the Southern Pacific was waged not only on the construction line. The halls of Congress, the houses of the state legislature, the courts of state and nation were all battlegrounds for the two forces. Throughout the 1870's, both companies sought aid in Congress. Seriously weakened by the financial panic of 1873, Scott wanted the federal government to underwrite the interest of his company's bonds. Huntington worked to prevent this by telling congressmen that his company would build a transcontinental line along the 32nd parallel without any financial subsidy, on condition that Scott's land grant would be handed over to it. Congress listened to both sides and did nothing, a situation that helped Huntington more than his adversary. For although financially pressed throughout the decade, the Big Four al-

Tom Scott was considered a threat to the expansion of the Southern Pacific. Scott first won fame in railroad management during the Civil War. He later directed the Texas Pacific's attempt to stop the progress of the Southern Pacific. — HUNTINGTON LIBRARY — SAN MARINO, CA.

ways managed to find the credit to push forward construction, while Scott, needing the federal guarantee to make his bonds salable, failed to move his tracks west of Texas. "Every mile that we build weakens Scott and strengthens us," Huntington wrote his friends.[12]

However, the Big Four were not invulnerable. Throughout the seventies, Scott's allies in Congress demanded the Central Pacific repay the federal loans of the previous decade. In 1878 this pressure materialized into the Thurman Act, which called for five percent of the annual net earnings of the Central Pacific for retiring the subsidy bonds. Scott had benefited from Janus-faced friends of the Big Four. Senator Aaron A. Sargent, an old political workhorse for Huntington in Washington, D.C., temporarily rebelled in the middle 1870's, giving the Justice Department arguments why the Central Pacific should be immediately compelled to repay its loan. Alfred A. Cohen, a former high-ranking employee of the Big Four, embarrassed them in 1876 by generating several stockholder's suits and lobbying in the California legislature for a railroad regulation bill, which if passed would have cut into the financial resources of the Central Pacific. But neither Sargent, Cohen, nor Scott could stop the progress of the Southern Pacific, which was completed to Los Angeles on September 5, 1876.[13]

119

Reaching the towering Tehachapi Mountains, the rails of the Southern Pacific came to an abrupt halt in 1874 as they tried to reach southern California. Here engineers faced the problem of raising the railroad 2,734 feet from the San Joaquin Valley floor at Caliente to the top of the mountain pass, an elevation of 4,025 feet in 16 miles as the crow flies. This feat was accomplished by swerving 28 miles of tracks in serpentine fashion around gradual curves of 2.2 percent grade through 18 tunnels. At one point, known as the Tehachapi Loop, the track looped over itself in a remarkable stroke of engineering. The Loop has since become one of the seven wonders of the railroad world. In the view above, an 1875 vintage train prepares to enter tunnel 10 between Walong and Marcel. — DONALD DUKE COLLECTION (OPPOSITE PAGE) A pair of woodburning steam locomotives on the Loop in 1876 when trains first operated over the new line linking Los Angeles with San Francisco. — SOUTHERN PACIFIC COLLECTION

Boring the San Fernando Tunnel, was the greatest single task the Southern Pacific had to complete in order to reach Los Angeles. The 6,966-foot bore, attacked from both ends simultaneously, was also shafted from the center. — WRIGHTWOOD COLLECTION

In entering Los Angeles from the north, the Southern Pacific built the 6,966-foot San Fernando tunnel, five times longer than the longest tunnel of the Central Pacific through the Sierra. Los Angeles's subsidy paid for only a scant fraction of the construction costs through the mountains north of the city. Interestingly enough, when the Big Four had become fully aware of the extreme difficulty of building through this terrain only months before the subsidy vote, they had considered sabotaging the election to free them to by-pass Los Angeles by building over an easier route through Cajon Pass and San Bernardino to the Colorado River. But rather than wed Los Angeles to Scott, the Southern Pacific had eventually worked for its subsidy victory and adhered, with some regret, to keeping Los Angeles on its main line. Not in a philanthropic mood following this experience, the Big Four charged Angelinos high rates for many years thereafter to compensate for their own sacrafice in "reclaiming Los Angeles to civilization."[14]

Understandably, residents of San Bernardino were disappointed that the Southern Pacific chose to enter southern California through the expensive San Fernando tunnel rather than their own Cajon Pass. Nevertheless, the Southern Pacific would be forced to come within a few miles of San Bernardino as it built eastward from Los Angeles toward San Gorgonio Pass and Arizona. Hence, San Bernardinians retained their optimism that their town would inevitably become a key rail center for southern California. "God made San Bernardino a site for the central town of the valley," proclaimed the *San Bernardino Argus,* "and the railroad, if inclined, and we have no reason to believe it to be, cannot change His fiat." Imbued with this attitude, San Bernardino refused to subsidize the Southern Pacific. The Big Four did not waste words. Left to their own resources, "they could not afford to swerve their line to the right or to the left to accommodate any little town." And they built their railroad five miles south of San Bernardino, creating the town of Colton in 1875 to serve as the depot for the San Bernardino area. If it was any comfort to San Bernardinians, their experience with the Southern Pacific was not unique. Stockton had similarly failed to achieve its dream of a railroad junction. Visalia in Tulare County had been left off the main line for its failure to subsidize the company. Bakersfield had been slighted in favor of Sumner (East Bakersfield) for the same reason, and the town of Tehachapi had been bypassed three miles to the east, for its 200 inhabitants did not warrant even a slight change of route. Hard-pressed in their race with Scott for a commercial empire, the Big Four often treated small towns with unceremonious dispatch.[15]

As the Southern Pacific made steady progress first into Los Angeles and then eastward past San Bernardino and toward San Gorgonio Pass, San Diegans grew increasingly impatient with the inactivity of Scott. A few of them even broached the possibility of an alliance with the Southern Pacific. Quickly the Big Four moved to add San Diego to their southern California chorus by promising to build San Diego's long-desired connection with Yuma. Although unhappy with Scott's performance, most San Diegans saw the Southern Pacific's proposition as the notorious spider's parlor. By deserting Scott, San Diego would throw away its hope of commercially defeating San Francisco, for unfailingly the Big Four would

THE "LOOP" ROUTE

BUY YOUR TICKETS ONLY AT THE RAILROAD TICKET OFFICES and be sure they read via

thus saving time and expense, and avoiding the "Risks" and "Seasickness" incident to Ocean Routes.

Map of the
SOUTHERN PACIFIC
RAILROAD
CONNECTING WITH
CENTRAL PACIFIC R.R.
AT GOSHEN,
Sept. 5th 1876.

Examine Carefully the "Time Schedules" on reverse side for Trains via "Lathrop."

Reaching Los Angeles in September of 1876, the Southern Pacific continued its march toward Yuma and the Colorado River. At this time the Southern Pacific Railroad was popularly known as *The Loop Route*. Note the proposed extension to San Diego from Anaheim, and the coast line connection with the San Joaquin Valley route over Polonio Pass. At the time this map was printed, the rails had reached Indian Wells, now known as Indio, with 115 more miles of track required to reach Yuma. — DONALD DUKE COLLECTION

With the crossing of the Colorado River at Yuma, the Southern Pacific demonstrated a commanding superiority over the Texas Pacific in the race to control the first southern transcontinental line. — SOUTHERN PACIFIC COLLECTION

discriminate in favor of the latter city to encourage the long haul. "Stand by Scott; for he has stood by us," admonished the *San Diego Union*. "Let no *new* trades be made until we see clearly that the old one cannot be carried out."[16]

Having spurned the Big Four, San Diego sadly watched the march of the Southern Pacific through the San Gorgonio Pass to Ft. Yuma on the Colorado River, the western bank of which was reached in May 1877. There all progress was halted for several months by Scott, who protested to the federal government that his company's right to a land grant in Arizona would be prejudiced by the Southern Pacific's bridging of the river. With the Texas Pacific no farther west than Fort Worth, Texas, the Southern Pacific felt justified in illegally laying track across the Colorado, a deed done under the cloak of night. Faced with this accomplished fact as well

125

as local Arizona interests that wanted immediate rail facilities, the federal government consented to the Southern Pacific's crossing of the Colorado. And construction across the territory began. Even without the guarantee of acquiring the Texas Pacific's land grant, something which the Big Four would never receive, the Southern Pacific continued its construction eastward. Scott was beaten. In early 1877, Republican leaders promised him a federal subsidy as part of the North-South deal that gave the Presidency to Rutherford B. Hayes, but the pledge was later violated. By the end of the decade, reporters were noting that the railroad king was "prematurely worn out." San Diegans were less kind to the leaders of the Texas Pacific in defeat. "They have been weak and stupid," wrote one citizen. "This is the only conclusion an unbiased man can arrive at." By 1880, the Big Four's track extended to Tucson; by 1881, to El Paso, and on to New Orleans, which was reached in January 1883.[17]

San Diegans were crestfallen. Nevertheless, they enjoyed the satisfaction of knowing that Los Angeles did not meaningfully share in the Southern Pacific's triumph. For shortly after the Big Four won their race to the Colorado River, they eradicated all sea competition between San Francisco and Los Angeles by strategic rate cutting, causing one influential citizen of Los Angeles to claim that some transportation costs had actually been less before the coming of the railroad. Such talk was dismissed by Charles Crocker as mere "blatherskiting." "The Los Angeles people are trying to make us trouble," wrote David Colton to Huntington, "because the railroad has not made them all rich, and has not caused rain this season to make good crops." Added to Los Angeles's bitterness was the realization that an earlier warning of a *San Diego World* editorial was coming true. "The very instant Stanford's road is completed," the newspaper had prophesied, "Los Angeles will enjoy the happiness of being a way station on the route to Yuma. The San Francisco drummers will alight there for a little refreshment on their way to San Bernardino, Yuma and nothern Arizona." The volume of criticism rose in other southern California localities as they came fully to realize that they were "nothing but convenient appendages to the one great city of the State," existing merely "to enhance the colossal wealth of the Babylon of the Pacific coast."[18]

One key factor kept rates high in southern California. The railroad had been built to the area before local business conditions really warranted it.[19] The overriding goal of the Big Four in their rapid construction southward had been to beat the Texas Pacific. Nevertheless, Angelinos refused to see why they should pay the maintenance costs of the Big Four's California monopoly. By the end of the 1870's, they had become the loudest critics of the Southern Pacific.

Anti-railroad feeling was not restricted to the southern part of the State. Even before the completion of the Central Pacific, movements began to arise in northern California to cut the flow of public largess to railroad companies and lower their rates by state action. Communities responded to these movements at different times. As the example of Los Angeles illustrates, most communities failed to join the attack on the monopoly until after they received railroad facilities. Such anti-railroad agitation would meet with uneven success, but that is the story of several of the following chapters.

NOTES

1. *Chicago Tribune,* Sept. 8, 1869 (found in Bancroft Scraps [Bancroft Library, University of California, Berkeley], LXXX, 1309); unidentified newspaper, Feb. 6, 1872 (found in Bancroft Scraps, LXXX, 962); James McCague, *Moguls and Iron Men, The Story of the First Transcontinental Railroad* (New York, 1964), pp. 255-256.
2. *San Diego World,* Oct. 23, 1873 (found in Bancroft Scraps, LXXX, 519); *San Diego Union,* Aug. 27, 1872 (found in Bancroft Scraps, LXXX, 466); *ibid.,* May 5, 1874 (found in Bancroft Scraps, LXXX, 1267).
3. Franklyn Hoyt, "Railroad Development in Southern California, 1868-1900" (Unpublished doctoral dissertation, University of Southern California, 1951), pp. 289-293; Hubert Howe Bancroft, *History of California* (San Francisco, 1890), VII, 593-594; *Daily Alta California,* Aug. 21, 1868 (found in Bancroft Scraps, LXXX, 358).
4. Collis P. Huntington, *Letters from Collis P. Huntington to Mark Hopkins, Leland Stanford, Charles Crocker, E. B. Crocker, Charles F. Crocker, and David D. Colton* (New York, 1892-1894), I, 178-179, 292; James Guinn, *A History of California and an Extended History of Its Southern Coast Counties* (Los Angeles, 1907), I, 222; George Tinkham, *History of San Joaquin County, California* (Los Angeles, 1923), pp. 250-251.
5. The Lewis Publishing Co., *In Illustrated History of San Joaquin County, California* (Chicago, 1890), p. 135; Tinkham, *San Joaquin County,* pp. 253, 356-358.
6. Lewis B. Lesley, "A Southern Transcontinental Railroad into California: Texas and Pacific Versus Southern Pacific, 1865-1885," *Pacific Historical Review,* V (1936), 52-54; *San Diego World,* Dec. 15, 1872 (found in Bancroft Scraps, LXXX, 502).

7. James Guinn, *Historical and Biographical Record of Southern California from its Earliest Settlement to the Opening Year of the Twentieth Century* (Chicago, 1902), p. 139.

8. Guinn, *A History of California*, I, 318-319; *Los Angeles Evening Express,* Aug. (day unknown), 1871 (found in Bancroft Scraps, LXXX, 398); *San Diego Union,* Sept. 29, 1869 (found in Bancroft Scraps, LXXX, 958); *San Diego World,* Oct. 24, 1872 (found in Bancroft Scraps, LXXX, 491-492); *Daily Alta California,* Sept. 5, 1872, 1:8.

9. *San Diego World,* Nov. 7, 1872 (found in Bancroft Scraps, LXXX, 192).

10. *Daily Alta California,* May 7, 1873 (found in Bancroft Scraps, LXXX, 509); *San Diego World,* Oct. 23, 1873 (found in Bancroft Scraps, LXXX, 518); *ibid.,* Sept. 4, 1873 (found in Bancroft Scraps, LXXX, 516).

11. Delta Printing Establishment, *The Struggle of the Mussel Slough Settlers for their Homes! An Appeal to the People* (Visalia, 1880), pp. 11-14; Irving McKee, "Notable Memorials to Mussel Slough," *Pacific Historical Review,* XVII (1948), 19-27; *San Francisco Bulletin,* July 28, 1876 (found in Bancroft Scraps, LXXX, 572).

12. *San Diego Union,* Oct. 23, 1973 (found in Bancroft Scraps, LXXX, 1266); *Sacramento Record-Union,* Mar. 1, 1876, 4:2; Huntington, *Letters from Collis P. Huntington,* III, 449.

13. Stuart Daggett, *Chapters on the History of the Southern Pacific* (Berkeley, 1922), pp. 381-383; *San Francisco Bulletin,* Mar. 14, 1876 (found in Bancroft Scraps, LXXX, 837); *ibid.,* Sept. 7, 1876 (found in Bancroft Scraps, LXXX, 575); *Sacramento Record-Union,* Feb. 28, 1876, 2:2; *In the District Court of the Fourth Judicial District, of the State of California, in and for the city and county of San Francisco. John R. Robinson, Plaintiff, vs. the Central Pacific Railroad Company of California et al., Defendants. Complaint,* [By] *Alfred A. Cohen, Delos Lake, Attorneys for Plaintiff.* (San Francisco, 1876), p. 6.

14. William Hyde to Mark Hopkins, July 27, 1872, Mark Hopkins to William Hyde, Aug. 2, 1872, Huntington MSS (microfilm, Huntington Library, San Marino, Calif.); *Daily Alta California,* Jan. 26, 1875 (found in Bancroft Scraps, LXXX, 556-557); *San Francisco Bulletin,* July 15, 1876 (found in Bancroft Scraps, LXXX, 571).

15. Luther A. Ingersoll, *Ingersoll's Century Annals of San Bernardino County, 1769 to 1904* (Los Angeles, 1904), p. 255; Paul E. Vandor, *History of Fresno County, California, With Biographical Sketches* (Los Angeles, 1919), p. 178; Kathleen E. Small and J. Larry Smith, *History of Tulare County and Kings County, Calif.* (Chicago, 1926), pp. 162-167; Wallace M. Morgan, *History of Kern County, California* (Los Angeles, 1914), pp. 89-90.

16. *San Francisco Bulletin,* Aug. 14, 1875, 3:4; San Diegans often referred to the Southern Pacific as "Stanford's San Francisco railroad." See *San Diego News,* Feb. 24, 1878, 1:2; *San Diego Union,* Aug. 18, 1875 (found in Bancroft Scraps, LXXX, 559-560).

17. Hoyt, "Railroad Development in Southern California," p. 221; Mark Hopkins et al., *Letters from Mark Hopkins, Leland Stanford, Charles Crocker, Charles F. Crocker, and David D. Colton, to Collis P. Huntington. From Aug. 27, 1869 to Dec. 30, 1879* (New York, 1891), pp. 135, 137; Lesley, "A Southern Transcontinental Railroad into California," *Pacific Historical Review,* p. 60; *San Francisco Bulletin,* May 1, 1880 (found in Bancroft Scraps, LXXX, 622); Lewis B. Lesley, "The Struggle of San Diego for a Southern Transcontinental Railroad Connection, 1854-1891" (Unpublished doctoral dissertation, University of California, Berkeley, 1933), p. 246; Neill C. Wilson and Frank J. Taylor, *Southern Pacific, The Roaring Story of a Fighting Railroad* (New

York, 1952), p. 239.

18. *Report of the Board of Commissioners of Transportation to the Legislature of the State of California* (Sacramento, 1877), p. 23; *Debates and Proceedings of the Constitutional Convention of the State of California, Convened at the City of Sacramento, Saturday, September 28, 1878* (Sacramento, 1881), I, 480; Hopkins et al., *Letters from Mark Hopkins,* p. 107; *Ellen M. Colton v. Leland Stanford et al., Testimony (Arguments in the Superior Court of the State of California, in and for the County of Sonoma, 1883-1884)* (n.p., n.d.), XV, 7519; *San Diego World,* Jan. 31, 1874 (found in Bancroft Scraps, LXXX, 527); *Los Angeles Weekly Express,* Feb. 16, 1878, 2:3; *San Luis Obispo Tribune,* Feb. 26, 1876, 3:4.

19. Daggett, *Southern Pacific,* p. 170.

PART
FOUR

Attempts at Governmental Control

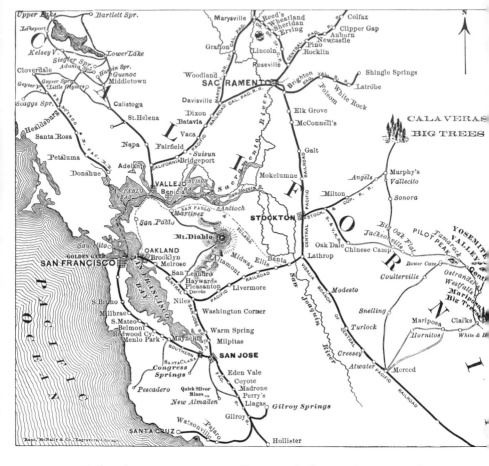

Railroad entreprenuers usually argued that track construction could not continue without local subsidies. Those communities not already served by the iron horse were the leaders opposing the movement to end an easy subsidy policy — a reform generally supported by towns having railroad facilities. The above map illustrates the bay area's rail network in the 1870's, when the subsidy issue was prominent on the California scene.

9

No More Subsidies

I N THE 19th century, state politics could affect California's railroad companies in several ways. For one, generous public subsidies could speed construction, not only by directly providing funds for that purpose but also by luring necessary European capital. The latter was especially needed for construction in California where local capitalists usually avoided railroad investments, preferring enterprises promising larger returns. On the other hand, foreigners could be satisfied with a more moderate rate of interest if they could be convinced that their investment was safe, something which public subsidies helped to secure.[1] Hence, California's railroad leaders could not afford to ignore state and local government, when so many fruits could be derived from them.

In regard to the Big Four's acquisition of state subsidies, California's constitution posed a major problem. The framers of the state's constitution of 1849 had outlawed state aid to railroad corporations, for they had wanted to insure that California would never repeat the foolish experiences of many eastern states a decade before when state bankruptcy had followed generous internal improvement subsidization. Correspondingly, they not only had created a constitutional ceiling on the state debt at $300,000, but also flatly barred the state from subsidizing corporations. But the Big Four later received state money in spite of these restrictions. The Civil War and the excitement of building the first transcontinental rail line encouraged Californians of the 1860's to temporarily ignore the words of their fathers, and state aid was lavishly expended on the Central Pacific. When appealed to the courts, these acts were invariably justified as war measures. However, this argument died with the surrender of the Confederacy's armies, and after 1865 California's governors required a more literal reading of the state constitution. Acquiescing, the Big Four ceased to seek financial assistance from the state.[2]

As a result, railroad corporations increased their pressure on counties for more subsidies. Since 1859, any county had been authorized to aid railroads with up to five percent of the assessed property values within its jurisdiction, as long as it first received the consent of the state legislature. But by 1870, such requests became so numerous that the legislature passed an act allowing counties to grant their bounty without having first to seek state approval. The resulting growth of county subsidies during the early seventies accentuated the already intense local rivalries of the day. As pamphleteer J. Ross Browne asked, how could the counties of the San Joaquin Valley withhold subsidies to hasten railroad facilities "when the spirit of progress is attracting immigration to other parts and to other States, possessing resources certainly not superior and a climate undoubtedly inferior?" If a community missed the opportunity to aid a beckoning corporation, the channels of trade would flow elsewhere, perhaps permanently.[3]

The story of St. Louis and Chicago was known by most Californians of this era. Chicago had been extremely energetic in promoting railroad facilities, while St. Louis, an older community operating in more cautious ways, had not pressed its advantages. The result? Chicago became the queen city of the Midwest. Statistics were used to prove the moral:

> In 1850 her population was 33,000, now [1866] it is over 200,000. In 1850 she had but forty miles of railroad running to the city; at present there is over 2,000. Twenty years ago but thirty-eight bushels of grain was exported; last year over 50,-000,000 were sent off. . . . It is a noticable fact that the States

and counties which are most liberal in loaning their credit to aid railroads, have become the most wealthy and prosperous; and those which refuse this aid, are poor and slow in growth.[4]

Thus, railroad promoters admonished communities not to fear a large public debt brought about by granting subsidies. The stock purchased by a county would eventually reap profits many times the purchase cost, enabling taxation to be considerably reduced and perhaps eliminated altogether. And the savings in transportation costs to farmers and merchants would make them all rich.[5]

But the condition of El Dorado County at that time seemed to belie these arguments. In the early 1860's, El Dorado County had given generously to schemes seeking to place Placerville on a transcontinental railroad. Those dreams had failed, but the debt accepted by the county in the struggle remained, accumulating interest. In addition, the decline of placer mining produced an exodus from the area later in the decade. But many heavy investors in El Dorado real estate did not leave, and they bore the tax burden created during a happier era.[6] Along with the experience of El Dorado County, other local complaints fostered a growing anti-subsidy mood. Quite often only one part of a county, actively interested in promoting local railroad facilities, would force unwanted subsidies on communities within the same county but far removed from the route. In addition, a railroad company would occasionally attempt to push a subsidy onto a county with results that won additional converts to the anti-subsidy cause. A blatant example of this occurred in 1868, when late in the legislative session a bill passed providing that Plumas County would give $230,000 of its bonds to the Oroville and Virginia Railroad. However, the act did not allow for a vote on the matter in the county. In order to foil what was seen in the county as a "grab" of its financial resources, the county board of supervisors resigned, thus leaving Plumas County without any representatives to issue the bonds. The matter was then taken to court, where after lengthy litigation the county won its fight. Publicity of this episode pointed up the potential injustices of the county subsidy system.[7]

In 1870, the anti-subsidy movement won an important ally in Governor Henry H. Haight, who vetoed several county subsidy bills that had passed the legislature. Although he did not then op-

135

Henry Haight

Henry George

Newton Booth

Henry Haight and Newton Booth were both anti-subsidy governors of California during the early 1870's. Henry George, later to become world-famous for his land tax prescription to end poverty, was in the early seventies a San Francisco newspaperman closely identified with the anti-subsidy forces. — WRIGHTWOOD COLLECTION

136

pose the passage of the general five percent subsidy law, he did call for its repeal in the following year. Holding to the axiom that the government that governs least governs best, Haight questioned whether a majority in an election had the right to encumber their neighbor's property with taxes to build a railroad. And above all, he warned his fellow Californians of the dangers to democratic government inherent in the county subsidy system.[8] The latter threat was especially stressed by Henry George, a San Francisco newspaperman and anti-subsidy pamphleteer later to win world fame as an economic theorist. Before it became too late, cautioned George, the easy method of acquiring county subsidies must be repealed, for soon the Central Pacific would be in a position to suck the resources of every county in the State. "This power, great as it is, is but in its beginnings," he prophesied. "A giant today, compared with what it was four years ago, it is yet an infant compared with what it will be four years hence."[9]

By 1872, the anti-subsidy movement was making headway in both state and nation. The Crédit Mobilier scandal of that year buried the possibility for future generous federal subsidies, and the Dolly Varden movement, also of that year, reflected strong anti-railroad feeling in California. Named after a calico print composed of many different colors and patterns, the Dolly Vardens were a conglomeration of liberal Republicans and Democrats anxious to bring railroad corporations under strict state regulations. Having elected Republican Newton Booth governor late in 1871, the Dolly Vardens succeeded the following year in partially repealing the general county subsidy act of 1870. Only partial repeal could be effected in 1872, as southern Californians were reluctant to enact a complete reform until they acquired railroad facilities. Although largely accepting the theories and arguments of the anti-subsidy movement, southern California's representatives suspected that the Dolly Varden agitation might be based partly on a desire of communities with railroads to prolong their artificial commercial advantages. Understandably then, the anti-subsidy legislation of 1872 exempted the counties of Los Angeles, San Diego, Santa Barbara, San Luis Obispo, San Bernardino, San Francisco, Santa Cruz, and Marin from its provisions. In 1872, even an anti-subsidy movement had to provide for an easy method for some counties to lure rail-

Pro-subsidy defenders argued that trains, such as this train somewhere in the San Joaquin Valley, could serve sparcely settled communities only if county subsidies were granted to encourage construction. — DONALD DUKE COLLECTION

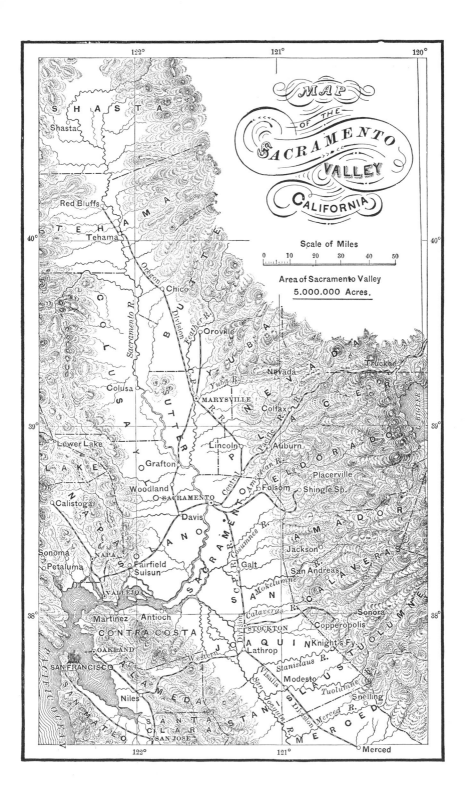

roads through their portals.[10]

In 1874, the law of 1870 was repealed completely. With railroad construction under way in several southern California counties, the fears of 1872 vanished. Nevertheless, some counties without railroads continued to petition the state legislature to authorize subsidy elections in their communities. This practice finally died out following the session of 1876-1877, when it became apparent that such legislation had no chance of success. But by that time, the Big Four had virtually perfected their monopoly, built in part by generous public subsidies. Public largess would be denied to all future challengers of the Big Four's California empire. Ironically, the reformers had indirectly aided that which they most despised.[11]

NOTES

1. *Daily Alta California,* June 10, 1870 (found in Bancroft Scraps, LXXX, 1319).
2. *Debates and Proceedings of the Constitutional Convention of the State of California. Convened at the City of Sacramento, Saturday, Sept. 28, 1878* (Sacramento, 1880), I, 8-9; *Daily Alta California,* Feb. 4, 1865, 2:1; *The Journal of the Assembly During the Sixteenth Session of the Legislature of the State of California, 1865-1866* (Sacramento, 1866), pp. 789-791; Stanford to Hopkins, May 30, 1867, Leland Stanford Correspondence (Stanford University Library, Stanford, California).
3. John Ross Browne, *The Policy of Extending Local Aid to Railroads, With Special Reference to the Proposed Line Through the San Joaquin Valley to the Colorado River* (San Francisco, 1870), p. 30; *Daily Alta California,* Jan. 29, 1870 (found in Bancroft Scraps [Bancroft Library, University of California, Berkeley], LXXX, 764); William C. Fankhauser, *A Financial History of California, Public Revenues, Debts, and Expenditures* (Berkeley, 1913), pp. 207, 211.
4. *Sonora Herald,* Feb. 17, 1866 (found in Bancroft Scraps, LXXX, 1091).
5. Browne, *The Policy of Extending Local Aid to Railroads,* pp. 38-40; Carter Goodrich, "The Revulsion Against Internal Improvements," *Journal of Economic History,* X (1950), 152.
6. *San Francisco Bulletin,* Oct. 29, 1873, 3:6; Fankhauser, *Financial History of California,* p. 223; Hubert Howe Bancroft, *History of California* (San Francisco, 1890), VII, 564.
7. *Sacramento Daily Union,* Aug. 5, 1870 (found in Stuart Daggett's California Railroad Notes [Bancroft Library, University of California, Berkeley], packet 24); George C. Mansfield, *History of Butte County, California* (Los Angeles, 1918), pp. 249-251, 267.
8. Henry H. Haight, *Message of Governor H. H. Haight, Returning Without Approval Senate Bills Nos. 243 and 244, Relative to Empower Certain Counties to Aid in the Construction of Railroads* (Sacramento, 1870), pp. 1-8.
9. Henry George, *The Subsidy Question and the Democratic Party* (n.p., 1871), pp. 2, 10, 11.
10. The Lewis Publishing Company, *An Illustrated History of Los Angeles County, California* (Chicago, 1889), pp. 135-136; Robert E. Riegel, *The Story*

of Western Railroads, From 1852 Through the Reign of the Giants (New York, 1926), p. 47; Fankhauser, *Financial History of California,* p. 211.

11. *San Francisco Bulletin,* Nov. 21, 1877 (found in Bancroft Scraps, LXXX, 1332); *ibid.,* Oct. 8, 1892, 1:4.

Frank Freeman

William Irwin

William Irwin (later to become Governor of California), as well as Frank Freeman and Lawrence Archer introduced the principal rate regulation measures in the California legislatures of the 1870's. Each measure had the defect of being too complicated for the average legislator to understand its overall impact upon California's railroad corporations. Nevertheless, most legislators were quite careful to discover what impact these proposals would have upon their constituent communities. Given this context, debates on bills amply demonstrated local ambitions and jealousies in railroad affairs. — WRIGHTWOOD COLLECTION

Lawrence Archer

10

The Movement to
Legislate Lower Rates

C OUNTY subsidies to railroad corporations were not the only
concerns of the Dolly Varden reformers. The passenger and
freight rates charged to the people of California were of far greater
importance and in fact had been a political issue in California
since its earliest years as a state, when ridiculously high rates had
been permitted in order to encourage railroad construction. An
act of 1853 had fixed the legal maximum for passengers at 20 cents
per mile and freight at 60 cents per ton mile, regulations that had
amounted to no regulation at all. In the following year, the legislature had reduced the maximums for passengers and freight to
ten and fifteen cents respectively, under the proddings of Governor
John Bigler, who had feared future corporations becoming "instru-
ments of extortion and oppression." These new levels were high
enough to encourage rapid development but not so high at that
time as to make a burlesque of public-carrier regulation. They
would remain the maximum rates for 22 years. But the longevity
of this schedule was not foreseen by the Big Four, who began to
fear reform movements to lower their rates after the Civil War.[1]

In 1865, these fears drove the Central Pacific to push for the
passage of new rate legislation in the form of a binding contract,

143

which could not be constitutionally withdrawn by subsequent legislatures. With the full support of the Central Pacific, a bill which would have lowered the legal maximum rates for areas at sea level and raised them for mountainous communities was introduced. It passed the legislature and was sent to the desk of Governor Frederick Low, where it was vetoed. "This bill, were it to become law," he admonished a naive legislature, "would clearly create a contract between the State and every company accepting its provisions — a contract that no subsequent legislature could repeal or impair." Not discouraged, Collis Huntington urged for another try in the following session. Late in 1867, he wrote to Charles Crocker: "If we could get the rates fixed so that the legislature could not change them, at about the present rates, it would be a great thing."[2] But the legislature was not likely to make the same mistake twice, and by 1868 some representatives — especially those from the mountainous counties of Placer, El Dorado, and Nevada — had begun to push for meaningful rate reduction. They attested that it cost less to ship a barrel of flour from Sacramento to Liverpool, England, than it did from California's capitol to their mountain homes. "Such rates of charges must be sensibly and promptly reduced," demanded one commentator. A *Placer Herald* editorial clearly reflected the anti-railroad feeling growing in the central Sierra: "The company was in limited circumstances, without adequate means to prosecute the work, when Placer, rich, out of debt and money to spare, came to its relief and placed it on the high road to wealth and fame, and now the company and its managers are exceedingly wealthy, and the county is poor, though she has been the heaviest contributing stockholder of all."[3]

Several bills to reduce rates were then introduced in both houses, causing Huntington to comment: "Everyone is in favor of a railroad until they get it built, and then everyone is against it, unless the railroad company will carry them and theirs for nothing."[4] Happily for Huntington, few communities had railroads. The Senate Committee on Corporations of that year recommended that the legislature "should not sacrifice the good faith and best interests of the state at large merely to cheapen railroad facilities to a few who are already well provided for, while other parts of the state are destitute of them." These railroad bills would retard, perhaps even prevent, construction of track to other areas of California. Likewise, the committee warned, they would weaken the Central Pacific in its race with the Union Pacific for commercial empire. The meeting at Promontory was still a year in the future, and nobody could predict the outcome. Largely for these considerations, all regulation bills were defeated in that session. When the legislature next met, the first transcontinental line had been completed, somewhat encouraging the movement to legislate lower rates. The company justified its high rates by claiming poverty, yet at that very time mansions were being constructed for the Big Four in Sacramento and New York. In the eyes of a few Californians, especially those in Placer County, the proper moment for rate reduction had arrived.[5]

However, the majority of Californians were not as yet interested in stringent railroad regulation. Their attitudes were reflected in the following statements by legislative committees recommending that rate regulation bills be defeated in 1870 and 1872:

Railroads are yet incomplete here. . . . Railroads are yet in their *creative* state. . . . Every energy and all means in this State are devoted to creating the firm basis and ground work of a railroad system upon which the innumerable future local developments can be made with proper economy to the State and attraction to foreign or eastern capital.[6]

A reduction of the present tariff would discourage the construction of new roads. It must be remembered that the Central Pacific Railroad has been constructed under the present law; and if that is liberal, any reduction made now would aid the road named to the discouragement of any road. A road now in operation could better afford to be controlled by a low tariff than a new road without an established business. This has been illustrated in the State of Illinois, where the low tariff was adopted after all railroads were constructed, and it had the effect to stop all further railroad construction. . . . It must not be forgotten that California has but one mile of railroad to two hundred and four square miles of territory, while New York possesses one mile to 11.9 square miles. Pennsylvania possesses one mile to 9.8 square miles. Ohio possesses one mile to 11.2 square miles. Illinois posseses one mile to 11.5 square miles. Missouri possesses one mile to 32.6 square miles. Massachusetts possesses one mile to 5.2 square miles.[7]

145

Local desires for railroad facilities had again saved the Big Four from unwanted regulation. However, by the summer of 1873, the Central Pacific's executives were genuinely upset about growing Dolly Varden agitation against them. "I would suggest that you see Stanford and Crocker and prepare for a wild, agrarian raid on us next winter," wrote a fearful Huntington to Mark Hopkins.[8]

The primary duty of defending the firm in Sacramento's legislative halls belonged to Leland Stanford, who had two very effective weapons at his disposal—money and convincing logic. Although he later swore under oath that he "never corrupted a member of the legislature," much circumstantial evidence supports the opposite conclusion. In fact, Collis Huntington himself would later confess that Stanford spent a total of $3,000,000 influencing legislation over the years. However, Stanford's political victories resulted from more than just corruption. Supplementing corrupt votes with honest ones was the method regularly employed by the Central Pacific. In an interview with Hubert Howe Bancroft in 1883, former Governor Frederick Low described the strategy commonly used during this period to defeat unwanted legislation: "You take a measure where there is *an honest difference of opinion* and then if you can get a minority of rascals to act solidly together [on] one side or the other, you can usually swing it." Before a federal investigating commission, Stanford himself later emphasized the role of logic in successful lobbying: "All those bills we were able to defeat. Every one of them helped to defeat itself. They were generally gotten up in malignity and by men who did not understand the subject, and whenever we could get such bills before a committee composed of fair-minded men, to whom we could explain the true nature and the necessary effect of such legislation, the bills helped to defeat themselves."[9]

The importance of local interests in the politics of regulation was pronounced in California, where population distribution was very uneven and geographical conditions varied. For example, the Sacramento Valley had a much greater population than the San Joaquin Valley.[10] Residents of the Sacramento Valley complained when a maximum freight and fare bill offered the same rate schedule for both valleys. Their greater population, they argued, entitled them to receive rates lower than those charged to the residents of

146

the San Joaquin Valley. When a bill proposed lower rates for valley than for mountain traffic, the mountain communities complained that the rate differential was too great.[11] If a bill was drawn giving the mountain regions rates suitable for the flat Sacramento Valley, then reasonable men opposed it as being unfair to the railroad companies. A maximum freight and fare bill, whatever its provisions, opened a Pandora's box of conflicting local interests, which were used by Central Pacific politicos in carrying out their strategy of divide and conquer. This policy was clearly exemplified in a statement made by Leland Stanford before the state senate committee reviewing various railroad rate bills in 1874. Stanford told the committee that he hoped that the people of California would not

> yield to any doctrine which forces upon communities an equality which nature never gave nor intended; which forces San Francisco, after the attainment of her commercial preeminence, to not only pay for all services rendered her individually, but to partially bear the burdens of Stockton, Sacramento, and Marysville; or which requires San Jose to draw from her pocket wherewith to build up Watsonville, Salinas, or Hollister; or for Sacramento to bear the direct results of the retrogression of El Dorado, in her diminished population and tonnage; or of the costliness of the mountain services to Placer and Nevada; or which requires Stockton to assume the partial cost of building Merced to sustain Plainsburg in existence; or that any of these places shall be required to take from their natural or artificial advantages arising from labored development, wherewith to build up and sustain those that nature or circumstances has left less favored and less fortunate.[12]

Maximum rate bills, such as the Freeman bill of 1873-1874, occasionally proposed to regulate rich and poor roads equally.[13] Such a policy seriously threatened people in areas served by financially weak roads. For example, the Freeman bill would have driven Peter Donahue's short line in Sonoma County into bankruptcy and forced it to suspend operations. Donahue's rate for merchandise shipped between Cloverdale in northern Sonoma County and San Francisco was $8.40; Freeman's bill, designed to regulate the Central Pacific, would allow Donahue only $2.70 between Cloverdale and San Francisco. In order to save his constituency's only road from bankruptcy, Sonoma County's state

147

senator joined the majority of the senate in opposing the Freeman bill.[14] The Archer bill, the principal maximum rate bill before the California legislature in 1875-1876, attempted to answer the Freeman bill's critics by proposing higher rates on roads under 50 miles in length.[15] But it too alienated representatives from counties with financially weak roads. For example, in Marin County, a narrow-gauge line called the North Pacific Coast Railroad was being built to connect Sausalito with Guerneville on the Russian River. Early in 1876, the road had reached Tomales, 55 miles from its terminus in the North Beach area of San Francisco. The road, therefore, would be subject to the lowest rates posted in the Archer bill. The vice president of the line complained before the senate committee reviewing the Archer bill that the measure ignored the special handicaps of his road. Although the bill authorized an advance in rates when a road reached an elevation of 1500 feet, it did not consider that the North Pacific Coast road contained many curves and steep grades under 1,500 feet elevation. Under the Archer bill, his road would also have to bear the same rates as roads traversing more heavily populated areas. Persuaded that the Archer bill would halt construction on the road, the senator from Marin County voted against the measure.[16]

Many representatives from counties without railroad facilities were also in opposition to the Dolly Varden rate reduction bills of the mid-seventies. For instance, in March 1874, when other counties were talking of railroad regulation, Santa Barbara townsmen were publicly trying to lure the Atlantic and Pacific Railroad to Santa Barbara. Santa Barbara's senator accordingly voted against stringent railroad regulation in 1874. On the other hand, Senator W. A. Eakin of Tuolumne, Inyo, and Mono Counties voted for the Freeman bill in the 1874 session.[17] At that time, no railroad projects were under way in his counties, nor were any contemplated. But by 1876, the Big Four were hinting at a road to connect Owens Valley in Inyo County with the Southern Pacific's main line. Hence, Senator Eakin listened closely to the logic of Leland Stanford, who spoke before the senate committee reviewing the Archer bill:

> How soon would the local line from Tehachapi to the mines of Cerro Gordo, Darwin, Panamint, and thence up to the Owens river valley, be built under restrictive legislation, which for the

Those favoring stringent railroad regulation drafted their proposals with the Big Four's monopoly in mind. Usually short lines such as the North Pacific Coast Railroad were insufficiently considered by authors of bills in the seventies because they were narrow gauge and made no physical connection with other carriers. This helped generate the needed opposition. In the view above, North Pacific Coast No. 4 is decorated for the 4th of July celebration in 1884. (BELOW) North Pacific Coast No. 6 at Mill Valley circa 1896. — BOTH GERALD M. BEST COLLECTION

first 125 miles precludes for the highest class of freight a charge of more than $7.50 per ton, for which is now paid over $80 per ton from Los Angeles and for the products of the mines and furnaces, but $4.50 per ton, for which at present over $40 per ton is being received for delivery by teams at Los Angeles?

Eakin voted against the Archer bill.[18] Like Eakin, Senator Robert McGarvey of Mendocino, Humboldt, and Del Norte Counties saw the conflict between the Archer bill and the interests of his constituency. The citizens of Ukiah in Mendocino County had offered Peter Donahue $60,000 to link their city with his northern terminus at Cloverdale, and he had been seriously considering their offer. However, if the low Archer rates were enacted, Donahue claimed that it would hardly be worth his while to build the road. Correspondingly, McGarvey voted against the Archer bill.[19]

If the representatives of small hamlets had been the only legislators opposing rate bills, stringent railroad regulation most certainly would have passed. Political power in the legislatures of the 1870's did not rest with them but rather in the urban delegations. Strong in the assembly and controlling as much as one-fourth of the state senate, San Francisco's local interests rivaled the Central Pacific as the single most powerful force in state politics.[20] Clearly, the unfriendliness of San Francisco's mercantile community to strict rate regulation in the seventies helps explain why such measures failed. San Francisco's merchants had good reasons to oppose maximum rate bills. Located at the primary competing point in the State, they enjoyed the lowest intrastate rates offered by the Big Four. And the Central Pacific's interstate rates also favored San Francisco, in order to encourage the long haul.[21] But, the Central Pacific warned, this discriminatory treatment might end if a false equality among communities were enforced by legislation. Desiring to maintain their advantageous competitive position, most San Francisco merchants opposed the Freeman bill in 1874.[22]

By the following year, San Francisco had an additional reason to oppose all rate reduction measures, for the Big Four were then engaged in their mad race with Tom Scott's Texas Pacific, which was allied to the commercial interests of St. Louis. The Archer bill, by cutting railroad revenues in California, would slow the momentum of the eastward-building Southern Pacific and might give

150

the trade of Arizona to the merchants of St. Louis. But more was involved than merely the trade of Arizona. Stanford warned that if the Southern Pacific did not reach the Colorado River first, San Francisco itself would fall to the invaders from St. Louis. Testifying before the state assembly committee on federal relations, he said: "I state here that if Scott comes to the Colorado River, the probabilities are that he will go to San Francisco. He will not build a line through the state, but he will offer such a price for a controlling interest in the Southern Pacific that his offer will not be refused."[23] The fight between the Big Four and Scott was a struggle to the death. Whichever company succeeded in controlling a southern transcontinental line would be able to force all rival lines into a subservient position or destroy them altogether. A southern line would traverse relatively flat land, untroubled by mountainous terrain and snow in the winter. A line from southern California to the Mississippi River and connected with the east coast by swift steamer would possess many commercial advantages over the Central Pacific. If Scott won the race, thus forcing the sale of the Southern Pacific, the Central Pacific would also go; for in 1876, Scott's ally, Jay Gould, controlled the Union Pacific. Should these two railroad barons control the entire length of a southern transcontinental line, they could so cripple the Central Pacific by control of its eastern connection and by competition over the southern line that the Central Pacific would inevitably fall into their hands.[24]

Because of fears generated by the above knowledge, seven of San Francisco's ten state senators opposed the Archer bill.[25] Frank McCoppin, the most vocal of the seven, said that he did not question the right of the state to regulate railroad rates. "They are," he declared, "mere pottery [sic] in the hands of the Legislature, to be molded from time to time into such forms as will meet the changing wants and necessities of the public." But he recognized that the Archer bill was not in the commercial interests of San Francisco:

It is for the interest of my constituents that the Southern Pacific Railroad should be extended as far east as possible, to the end that the commerce of the western portion of this continent may flow toward and be controlled by that city in which my home has been for so many years, and whose people have so distinguished me. The prosperity, the greatness of San Francisco, which is now and for years has been my highest, best ambition, would not be promoted by the passage of this bill.[26]

Not only the opponents of rate regulation bills were motivated by local self-interest. The primary spur of those California legislators supporting such legislation came from their communities as well. This can most clearly be seen by analyzing the benefits of the various bills under discussion. For example, the Freeman bill was framed to favor short-haul shippers. The region which would profit from this bill encompassed those counties within a 95-mile radius of San Francisco, an area which included Assemblyman Frank S. Freeman's Yolo County. The Irwin bill, another maximum rate bill in the 1873-1874 session, offered lower grain rates than did Freeman's bill for shipments of more than 95 miles. Senator William Irwin, author of the bill, represented Siskiyou County, a district more than 95 miles distant from the principal markets of the State.[27] Assemblyman Lawrence Archer of Santa Clara County framed his bill in part to protect a narrow-gauge project which was to connect several towns in his county. Roads under 25 miles in length, which would include the Santa Clara County narrow-gauge road, would be allowed to charge 20 cents per ton mile for freight, five cents higher than the current legal maximum. On the other hand, Archer's rates for merchandise shipped between San Francisco and Santa Clara County on the Big Four's road would be four cents per mile, considerably below the railroad's current rate. Grain and lumber merchants in Santa Clara County would also be able to ship their products for less money if Archer's bill passed. In short, the Archer bill was tailor-made for Santa Clara County.[28]

Representatives from some other counties found these bills suited to their local interests as well. Senator Tipton Lindsey of Fresno, Kern, and Tulare Counties early became an ardent supporter of the Archer bill. The Big Four charged their highest flat-land rates in his three sparsely settled counties. But in some respects high rates were justified in the lower San Joaquin Valley. In reporting against the Archer bill, the senate committee on corporations said: "The business on all stations of the Visalia division of the Central Pacific Railroad [in the San Joaquin Valley] was but one twenty-first of the business done on the western division of the same road, and but one-fifth of the business done on the Oregon division."[29] The amount of business, retorted the valley residents, was kept low by the high rates, a situation which the Archer bill promised to remedy. San Diegans also enthusiastically supported the Archer bill, for they were for any measure that would hurt the Southern Pacific in its race with Tom Scott. Correspondingly, San Diego's Assemblyman J. M. Pierce voted for the bill. Nevertheless, San Diego's and San Bernardino's joint senator, John W. Satterwhite, opposed the bill, following the wishes of his San Bernardino constituents who would profit from being located near the main line of the Southern Pacific.[30]

Like Senator Satterwhite, Senator William C. Hendricks represented a district with divided loyalties. His Lassen County constituents found the Archer bill an anathema, for in 1876 they were seriously considering a railroad extension to Reno, Nevada. This project, it was believed, would never get beyond the planning stage if the Archer bill passed, for the road would be over 50 miles in length and therefore not permitted to charge the higher rates allowed for short lines. The citizens of the county were also planning an 85-mile long railroad to connect the Sacramento River with the lumber region around Susanville. Hence, Assemblyman John S. Chapman of Lassen County supported the desires of his constituents when he voted against the Archer bill. But Senator Hendricks's Butte County supporters, with the Central Pacific passing through their territory, desired railroad regulation. The Archer bill met all the expectations of the farmers near Chico in Butte County. Under the bill, grain from around Chico would travel to market at rates below those currently charged by the Central Pacific.[31] No matter which way Hendricks cast his ballot he was certain to anger voters. Speaking before the senate, he stated: "Mr. President, on an important question like the present, a simple 'yes' or 'no' vote may give but an imperfect idea of the real sentiments of the voter — it may be but the resulting balance from a long sheet of pros and cons." He proceeded to criticize the Archer bill, calling it "arbitrary":

> There are two periods in the history of all countries in which capital is the central figure, though in opposite positions. First, when the country is new, to be sought, courted and encouraged

as a needed friend; and in the second, when the same capital, which has warmed it into life and prosperity, becomes aggressive and is to be watched. In every State these two conditions may, generally do, exist; and in every grade between the two extremes; therefore the same rules and laws cannot apply.[32]

Lassen County was in the first period described by Hendricks; Butte, in the second. He concluded his speech by saying that he would vote for the bill. Hendricks was accused by some of having made a confusing performance by first damning the Archer bill and then promising to vote for it. But far from being confused in his thinking, Hendircks was merely explaining to his Lassen County constituents that his decision had not been an easy one to make.

Representatives from Los Angeles likewise were denied a situation of easy choices. Angelinos were directly involved in the race between the Southern Pacific and Tom Scott. But unlike San Franciscans, this struggle was not their sole concern, for they were also interested in the Los Angeles and Independence Railroad, which

Senator John P. Jones, director of the Los Angeles & Independence Railroad Company, vied with the Southern Pacific for loyalties of Los Angeles in the mid-seventies. — BANCROFT LIBRARY

A work train of the Los Angeles & Independence Railroad during construction of the road between Santa Monica and Los Angeles. The LA&I challenged the Southern Pacific for control of Cajon Pass in 1876. — GERALD M. BEST COLLECTION

had been incorporated in 1874 by the state legislature. The promoter of the project was United States Senator John P. Jones of Nevada. Although the official purpose of the road was to connect the city of Los Angeles with the town of Independence in Inyo County, it was well publicized that Jones planned to build through the Owens Valley and connect with the Utah Southern Railroad coming south from Salt Lake City. If the Jones project succeeded, Los Angeles would be the terminal city of a transcontinental railroad and not merely a wayside station. In 1876, the Southern Pacific and the Los Angeles and Independence Railroad were both battling for control of the strategic Cajon Pass, some 22 miles north of San Bernardino. If the Southern Pacific gained possession of the pass first, the Los Angeles and Independence project would be undone. Los Angeles and Independence backers reasoned that the Archer bill might so weaken the enemy that the battle of Cajon could be won. Also, the bill might halt the Southern Pacific's march toward Los Angeles, thereby driving the Angelinos supporting the Southern Pacific to back the Los Angeles and Independence as the city's only hope.[33]

The Archer bill, to be sure, was bitter medicine for the Los Angeles and Independence people to swallow, for their revenues would also be cut by its provisions. But it would injure the Southern Pacific more by regulating all the roads in the state controlled by the Big Four.[34] Jones, having no plans for extensive railroad construction within the state, knew that the Archer bill would apply only to the freight rates on shipments between Los Angeles and Inyo County. Through freights, traveling over his proposed transcontinental road, would not be affected. Jones drew capital to build the line from his mining operations in Nevada and therefore was not dependent upon the revenues derived from current freight tariffs. Believing that the bill would hurt his adversaries more than himself, he instructed his chief engineer, Joseph U. Crawford, to support the measure.[35]

But not all Angelinos viewed the railroad situation as did Senator Jones. In regard to the Archer bill, Assemblyman John R. McConnell from Los Angeles said:

> I feel deeply on this subject, Mr. Speaker, because what is called the Southern Pacific Railroad was intended in a few months to connect with the city of Los Angeles; and I do do [sic] fear, I dread, if an Act of this kind should pass, that the road will not be completed, according to the present programme. There is now a gap of 100 miles to fill, but in addition to that, that same company is engaged in extending the road eastward through the San Gorgonio Pass to the Territory of Arizona, and are making rapid progress.[36]

At this time, many Angelinos thought the success of the Southern Pacific would bring the trade of Arizona to their city instead of to San Francisco. Ocean steamers could ship eastern goods to Los Angeles cheaper than to San Francisco, and Los Angeles was closer to Arizona than was San Francisco. In March, the Los Angeles Chamber of Commerce passed a resolution condemning the Archer bill, and a petition opposing it was signed by many of the business leaders of the city. Closely linked to the belief that the bill might prevent the Southern Pacific from reaching Los Angeles was the fear that it would halt the speculative boom in real estate, caused by the expectation of railroad conections with the northern half of the State. "To have the building of these roads suddenly stopped," reasoned the *Los Angeles Herald,* "and the track now built rendered inoperative, is a blow to our prosperity that we can hardly stand. If Senator Archer had deliberately set about framing a bill that should do the greatest possible injury to Los Angeles and southern California, he could not have accomplished his purpose more effectively than he has in his freights and fares production." The division of feeling in Los Angeles County was manifested in the legislature. Assemblyman Frederick Lambourn and Senator C. W. Bush voted for the Archer bill; Assemblyman McConnell opposed it.[37]

The Freeman, Irwin, and Archer bills all failed passage. But one rate measure, the O'Connor bill, did pass in the 1876 session. This bill designated the currently charged rates as the new legal maximums. This was a reform of sorts for the current rates were generally lower than the legal maximum tariffs established in 1854. Passed by the legislature over the opposition of Leland Stanford, the O'Connor bill had the advantage of seriously offending no local interests. It also provided for the creation of a three-man commission, which would investigate railroad affairs in the State as a prelude to regulatory legislation which would lower existing rates.[38] The commissioners, appointed by the governor, were intelligent, honest men who undertook their task with an enthusiasm that troubled the Big Four. Failing to corrupt the commission, the directors of the Central Pacific turned their political energies to controlling the next legislature, due to meet in the winter of 1877-1878.[39]

In the past, stringent rate bills had been killed in the state senate, usually by the narrowest of margins. The Big Four liked to concentrate on the senate, the smallest of the two houses through which all legislation had to pass on the way to the governor. But in the senate of 1877, the Central Pacific would not have to worry about close victories, for as Stanford wrote Huntington that fall: "The legislature elected is I think a good one and I apprehend less trouble from it than from any preceding legislature for the last ten years — not a single unfriendly senator elected."[40] By the following year, this legislature had won recognition as "the most corrupt that ever convened in this State." All legislation recommended by the railroad commission was defeated, and the Hart Act, supported by the Big Four, passed into law. Replacing the commission created by the O'Connor Act with an emasculated one-man commission, the Hart Act also relieved the Southern Pacific of several lawsuits initiated by Los Angeles shippers. During its short existence, the O'Connor Act had greatly annoyed the Big Four. At the time of its passage, the Southern Pacific's rates in the Los Angeles area were at one-fifth their normal levels, due to competition from the Los Angeles and Independence Railroad. However, by early 1877 the Los Angeles and Independence was forced to sell out to its rival because of financial hardships, imposed both by the low rates and a depression that hit California late in 1876. Following the sale, the Southern Pacific illegally raised its rates in Los Angeles, producing the lawsuits later wiped away by the Hart Act which changed the legal maximum rates to those actually "in use" on January 1, 1878. The Big Four were once again fully in control.[41]

However, in their moment of triumph, the directors were haunted by a new specter. The depression previously mentioned had done more than just force the sale of the Los Angeles and Independence. Men were thrown out of work. A radical workingmen's movement arose, with laissez-faire capitalism and cheap Chinese labor as its chief targets. By the fall of 1877, an Irish orator named Denis Kearney was emerging as leader of the movement, which spawned a flourishing political party early the next year. This new Workingmen's Party would help shape California's reform-minded second constitution in 1878.

NOTES

1. *Debates and Proceedings of the Constitutional Convention of the State of California, Convened at the City of Sacramento, Saturday, Sept. 28, 1878* (Sacramento, 1880), I, 574; *Daily Alta California,* April 10, 1854, 2:4-7.
2. *Trustees of Dartmouth College v. Woodward,* 4 Wheaton 518 (1819); Robert Lively, "The American System: A Review Article," *Business History Review,* XXIX (1955), 90; *Journal of the California Senate, Sixteenth Session* (Sacramento, 1866), pp. 734-735; Collis P. Huntington, *Letters from Collis P. Huntington to Mark Hopkins, Leland Stanford, Charles Crocker, E. B. Crocker, Charles F. Crocker, and David D. Colton* (New York, 1892-1894), I, 63.
3. *Grass Valley Union,* Nov. (day unknown), 1867 (found in Bancroft Scraps [Bancroft Library, University of California, Berkeley], XXXII, 1); *Stars and Stripes,* Jan. 9, 1868 (found in Bancroft Scraps, LXXX, 673); *Placer Herald,* (month and day unknown), 1868 (found in Stuart Daggett's California Railroad Notes [Bancroft Library, University of California, Berkeley], packet 24).

4. Huntington, *Letters from Collis P. Huntington*, I, 162. Compare Huntington's quote with a statement of an official of the Illinois Central, made during the same era: "The people are in favor of building a new road and do what they can to promote it. [But] after it is once built and fixed, then the policy of the people is usually in opposition." See Robert H. Wiebe, *The Search for Order, 1877-1920* (New York, 1967), p. 46.

5. "Majority Reports of the Committee on Corporations in Regard to Fares and Freights on Railroads," *Appendix to Journal of Senate and Assembly of the Seventeenth Session of the Legislature of the State of California* (Sacramento, 1868), II, Doc. 9, pp. 3-5; unidentified newspaper, July 17, 1869 (found in Bancroft Scraps, LXXX, 755-756); *New York Tribune,* (month and day unknown), 1869 (found in Bancroft Scraps, LXXX, 1217); Huntington, *Letters from Collis P. Huntington,* II, 59.

6. "Majority Report of the Committee on Corporations Relative to Senate Bill No. 62," *Appendix to Journals of Senate and Assembly of the Eighteenth Session of the Legislature of the State of California* (Sacramento, 1870), II, 3.

7. *Report of the Committee on Corporations of the Assembly of the State of California Upon Railroad Freights and Fares* (Sacramento, 1871), pp. 29-30.

8. Huntington, *Letters from Collis P. Huntington*, III, 18.

9. *Testimony Taken by the United States Pacific Railway Commission, Appointed Under the Act of Congress Approved March 3, 1887, Entitled 'An Act Authorizing an Investigation of the Books, Accounts, and Methods of Railroads Which Have Received Aid from the United States, and For Other Purposes'* (Washington, 1887), V, 2535; VI, 3170, 3258-3261; *San Francisco Examiner,* May 14, 1898, 14:2; Frederick F. Low, *Reflections of a California Governor* (Sacramento, 1959), p. 47.

10. In 1874, the population of the Sacramento Valley was 107,857; of the San Joaquin Valley, 69,000 (*Transactions of the California State Agricultural Society* [Sacramento, 1874], 226-227).

11. *Journal of the Senate of the State of California, Twentieth Session* (Sacramento, 1874), 758-759; *Sacramento Record-Union,* Mar. 28, 1876, 1:3-4; *San Francisco Bulletin,* Jan. 24, 1874, 4:1; Mar. 11, 1874, 2:1.

12. *Report of the Testimony and Proceedings Had Before the Senate Committee on Corporations, Having Under Consideration the Subject of Fares and Freights* (Sacramento, 1874), pp. 20-21.

13. For a detailed description of the Freeman bill, see *San Francisco Bulletin,* Jan. 15, 1874, 1:3.

14. *Report of the Testimony and Proceedings,* p. 63.

15. For a a detailed description of the Archer bill, see *San Francisco Bulletin,* Feb. 28, 1876, 1:1-3.

16. *Railroad Fares and Freights, Reports of the Senate Committee on Corporations, on Senate Bills Nos. 332, 319, and 334, and Assemby Bill No. 182* (Sacramento, 1876), pp. 5-6; *Sacramento Record-Union,* Mar. 23, 1876, 1-4.

17. T. H. Thompson and A. A. West, *Reproduction of Thompson and West's History of Santa Barbara and Ventura Counties, California* (Berkeley, 1961), p. 153; *San Francisco Bulletin,* Mar. 27, 1874, 4:1.

18. *Sacramento Record-Union,* Mar. 8, 1876, 8:7; Mar. 23, 1876, 1:4.

19. *Ibid.,* Mar. 8, 1876, 8:6; Mar. 23, 1876, 1:4; April 8, 1876, 3:1-7; *Railroad Fares and Freights, Report,* p. 40.

20. In the session of 1874, San Francisco had five senators; but in 1876, because of a reapportionment which gave the city more representation, San Francisco had nine senators and shared one with San Mateo County.

21. *San Francisco Chronicle,* Jan. 21, 1874, 2:1; *San Francisco Bulletin,* Jan. 22, 1874, 2:1; *Daily Alta California,* Sept. 12, 1872, 1:4-6.

22. In 1873, the San Francisco Chamber of Commerce proposed a railroad regulation plan rivaling the Freeman bill. Historians who have emphasized the role of merchants in the movement to regulate railroads have used this fact as a primary piece of supporting evidence. (See Gerald Nash, *State Government and Economic Development, A History of Administrative Policies in California, 1849-1933* [Berkeley, 1964], pp. 160-161.) However, the regulation plan sponsored by the San Francisco Chamber of Commerce was very mild. It merely proposed to eliminate "unjust" discrimination (open to judicial interpretation) between persons and places and to create a railroad commission to study the problem of railroad rates. Furthermore, the Chamber of Commerce committee concerned with railroad affairs warned against stringent maximum rate bills, like the Freeman bill: "Let us take heed, lest, in demanding security for the future, we cripple and disable thereby not only inflicting serious damage upon the state at large, but ultimately causing a reaction in favor of the monopoly." (See *San Francisco Bulletin*, Dec. 30, 1873, 1:1-4.)

23. *Sacramento Record-Union*, Feb. 29, 1876, 2:2; Mar. 7, 1876, 2:4-5; *San Francisco Bulletin*, Mar. 7, 1876, 2:3; Mar. 15, 1876, 2:1.

24. *Debates and Proceedings of the Constitutional Convention*, I. 502; Matthew Josephson, *The Robber Barons, The Great American Capitalists, 1861-1901* (New York, 1934), pp. 194-205; *Sacramento Record-Union*, Mar. 13, 1876, 1:6.

25. Only four of the ten San Francisco senators voted to table the Archer bill and a milder bill suggested by a San Francisco senator. Three of the six voting against the motion to table these bills were not for the Archer bill but rather for the milder substitute. Therefore, seven San Francisco senators opposed the Archer bill. (See *Sacramento Record-Union*, Mar. 23, 1876, 1:4.)

26. *Ibid.*, Mar. 22, 1876, 1:2-3.

27. *San Francisco Bulletin*, Mar. 16, 1874, 1:4.

28. Eugene T. Sawyer, *History of Santa Clara County, California* (Los Angeles, 1922), p. 151; *San Francisco Bulletin*, Feb. 28, 1876, 1:1-3.

29. Central Pacific Railroad Co., *Local Freight Tariff, June 22, 1873* (Hopkins Transportation Library, Stanford, California.); *Railroad Fares and Freights, Report*, p. 6.

30. *San Diego Union*, Mar. 19, 1876, 3:3; *San Bernardino Weekly Times*, Mar. 18, 1876, 2:1.

31. *San Francisco Bulletin*, Sept. 21, 1875, 2:3; *Sacramento Record-Union*, Feb. 26, 1876, 1:6; Mar. 8, 1876, 8:6; Compare the Archer bill's grain rate from Chico to San Francisco (see *San Francisco Bulletin*, Feb. 28, 1876, 1:1-3) with the Big Four's grain rate from Chico to San Francisco as posted in Southern Pacific Railroad Company's *Local Freight Tariff, To Take Effect January 1, 1875* (California State Archives, Sacramento).

32. *Sacramento Record-Union*, Mar. 21, 1876, 1:3.

33. *Statutes of California, 1873-1874* (Sacramento, 1874), pp. 772-773; Neill C. Wilson and Frank J. Taylor, *Southern Pacific, The Roaring Story of a Fighting Railroad* (New York, 1952), pp. 61-62; *Los Angeles Weekly Express*, Jan. 1, 1876, 1:4.

34. Collis P. Huntington wrote Charles Crocker in regard to the Archer bill: "The bill is an infamous one, and I hope you will be able to kill it. If we do not, I quite agree with you that we must stop all work, as we cannot run railroads in Cal., if it passes." (See *Letters from Collis P. Huntington*, III, 471.)

35. *Los Angeles Weekly Express*, Mar. 25, 1876, 2:4.

36. *Sacramento Record-Union*, Mar. 6, 1876, 4:1-3.

37. *Los Angeles Weekly Express,* April 1, 1876, 1:2; Carl B. Swisher, *Motivation and Political Technique in the California Constitutional Convention, 1878-1879* (Claremont, Calif.; 1930), pp. 46-47; *Sacramento Record-Union,* Feb. 26, 1876, 1:6; Mar. 19, 1876, 8:5; Mar. 23, 1876, 1:4; the quote from the *Herald* was reprinted in the *Record-Union,* Mar. 10, 1876, 3:5.
38. Ward McAfee, "Local Interests and Railroad Regulation in Nineteenth Century California" (Doctoral dissertation, Stanford University, 1966), pp. 68-74.
39. *Ellen M. Colton v. Leland Stanford et al., Testimony, Arguments in the Superior Court of the State of California, in and for the County of Sonoma, 1883-1884* (n.p., n.d.), IV, 1757; *Debates and Proceedings of the Constitutional Convention,* II, 641.
40. Mark Hopkins et al., *Letters from Mark Hopkins, Leland Stanford, Charles Crocker, Charles F. Crocker, and David D. Colton, to Collis P. Huntington, From August 27, 1869 to December 30, 1879* (New York, 1891), p. 119.
41. *Debates and Proceedings of the Constitutional Convention,* I, 574; *San Francisco Chronicle,* Mar. 20, 1878, 3:5; Mark Hopkins et al., *Letters from Mark Hopkins,* p. 191; *San Francisco Bulletin,* Dec. 16, 1875, 1:5; Franklyn Hoyt, "Railroad Development in Southern California, 1868 to 1900" (Doctoral dissertation, University of Southern California, 1951), pp. 51-84.

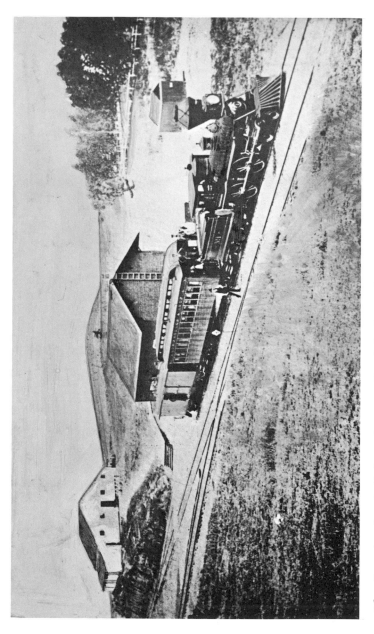

The Los Angeles & Independence Railroad had served as a rival to the Southern Pacific until its sale to the latter company in 1877. The following year, California's constitutional delegates met determined to harness the growing railroad monopoly. In this scene, an LA&I train prepares to leave Santa Monica for Los Angeles. — SECURITY-PACIFIC BANK COLLECTION

162

11

Constitutional Reform

I T IS A curious fact that the legislature of 1877-1878, which was the one most obviously dominated by railroad power during the 1870's, called into being a constitutional convention noted for its hostility to the Big Four. Actually, it had little choice in the matter. The preceding session of 1875-1876 had authorized a referendum on the need of a new constitution for California. The popular vote of September 5, 1877, being affirmative, the following railroad-controlled legislature dutifully passed the enabling act, which provided for the election of delegates in June 1878 and the assembling of the convention, which occurred in late September.[1]

The railroad directors most likely realized that there was less opportunity to influence the convening delegates than had been true for past legislators. There were several reasons for this. First of all, the obvious corruption of the immediately preceding legislature gave credence to the Big Four's critics who had long stressed that unregulated corporations were dangerous to democratic government. Secondly, the current economic depression made the public more hostile toward the Central Pacific than in previous years. White workingmen tended to blame the Central Pacific for the presence of low-wage Chinese competition in the state, for the

Anti-Chinese feeling was high in the late 1870's, and many disliked the railroad monopoly for drawing the orientals to California. This hurt the Southern Pacific's chances in the 1878 convention. — BANCROFT LIBRARY

company had imported thousands of Chinese in the sixties to work on the construction of its road. The wealth of the Big Four did not serve to make them popular either, at a time when many were without necessities. In addition, the structure of the convention simply worked against railroad influence. In legislative sessions, the railroad had concentrated its power in the senate, a body composed of 40 members. There, the company had blocked inimical legislation by corrupting and/or using logrolling techniques on roughly one-fourth of the upper house, while winning over another fourth by appealing to the local interests of various senators.[2] But how could the Central Pacific successfully use such tactics to control the constitutional convention, consisting of 152 members? Bribing up to one-fourth of the delegates would have proved to be very expensive, assuming such a large number could have been corrupted. Logrolling also could not be resorted to successfully in the convention, for it could only work if the opponents of the Central Pacific were relatively unorganized. But this prerequisite did not exist, for early in the convention the 51 Workingmen delegates caucused and pledged to operate as a radical unit. There was one final handicap for the Big Four. Unlike legislatures, held regularly every two years, constitutional conventions were extremely rare occurrences. Whereas a legislator could secretly "sell out," a convention delegate was very much aware of the public attention fixed upon him. While the state kept only spotty records of the happenings in the two houses of the legislature, a complete transcript of the debates of the constitutional convention was to be published at state expense. Publicity would strengthen the morally weak when confronted with pressure from the railroad. Realistically recognizing that the chances for control were remote, Leland Stanford decided to make no attempt to control the convention. In this situation, optimism was his sole resort. "It is the general opinion," Stanford wrote Huntington, "that what the convention will submit to the people will not be adopted."[3]

Early in their deliberations, the delegates began to discuss the several ways of regulating railroads. In past legislative sessions, men had argued endlessly over specific rates and examined particular bills to see if rates would be raised or lowered for their constituent communities. In the constitutional convention, on the other

165

hand, argument focused not on specific rates but on the various *methods* of regulating railroads, for a sizable number of the delegates challenged the notion that a legislative rate bill was the best method of regulation. They blamed conflicting community interests for past legislative failures on the subject. For these delegates, a railroad commission was the proper body to do the job. "Allow me to say, right here, that I am not one of those who believe that the legislature is necessarily corrupt, or that the people will knowingly send bad men to represent them in the legislature," said one delegate favoring a railroad commission with rate-setting powers.

> But I do argue — and I argue upon the basis, in the light of experience — that representatives coming from different localities in the State have their different local interests in charge, put those interests foremost in their endeavors to serve their local constituency, and combinations are nearly always formed in order to carry out these local enterprises. Now, if we leave this matter in the hands of the legislature, the railroad corporations will necessarily combine with these local interests, and this has been done over and over again to carry their schemes through, or to hamper and hinder legislation on this subject.[4]

A delegate opposing the commission idea acknowledged the truth of this history but challenged the conclusions drawn from it: "Years ago I said that we never could regulate this question, never could correct these abuses, until a majority of the counties of this state had these railroad corporations to deal with, and then we would find a clear working majority, without regard to parties, in favor of limiting and controlling this immense corporation." He concluded that with the construction of the Southern Pacific through the southern part of the state, fewer and fewer localities would oppose regulation in the future. Hence, the experience of past legislative sessions could not accurately forecast the future.[5] Pro-commission delegates countered with an effective argument. Railroad rate structures were immensely complex and far beyond the ken of the average legislator. In short, railroad regulation was an affair for experts. This argument proved to be most persuasive, and the convention decided to charge a three-man railroad commission with the power to set maximum rates. California was not the first state to create a commission with the power to set maximum rates.

166

However, it became the first to provide for such a commission in its state constitution. Here was a significant innovation. Other states might alter or repeal stringent regulation by railroad-influenced legislative enactment.[6] In California, the legislature would be bound to recognize the new regulation as part of the state's fundamental law. Ironically, this safeguard of the reformers of 1878-1879 would later become a major obstacle for reformers in years to come, for henceforth change could result only through the difficult amending process.

The powers granted to the railroad commission were broad. In addition to having the power to lower rates, it would have the sole power to raise rates lowered by competition. Its rates also were to be regarded as *conclusively* just and reasonable. In other words, the new constitution stated that there would be no judicial review of rates established by the California Railroad Commission. In many midwestern states, reformers had allowed for judicial review of the reasonableness of rates set by state rate-making authorities. But California's convention delegates, fearful of the Big Four's influence in the courts, broke with these precedents. The new constitution also provided that the three commissioners would be elected simultaneously by separate districts, insuring a public review of the rate-makers, something that would be compromised if courts were allowed to rule on the reasonableness of rates. The convention considered staggering the elections so that each commission would always have two members with a backlog of experience and knowledge in railroad affairs. But fear of the Southern Pacific "colonizing" voters in each district for the purposes of controlling all of the commissioner elections led the convention to decide to hold all three elections at the same time.[7]

The delegates concluded their efforts by writing a poorly drawn anti-discrimination section into the new constitution. The railroad commission was bound to eliminate *all* discrimination between persons or places. Literally, the prohibition of *all* discrimination between places would make the charge for a certain tonnage of freight for 50 miles exactly one-half of the amount charged for the same freight shipped 100 miles. But an unnecessary long-and-short-haul clause followed the prohibition against all discrimination, thus making the whole section somewhat ambiguous. Obviously, a

167

clause prohibiting higher charges for short hauls than longer hauls in the same direction was superfluous considering the earlier prohibition of all discrimination.

Finishing its labors, the convention sent its work to the people for ratification at a time when the Central Pacific was least prepared to fight it. Mark Hopkins had died in March 1878 while inspecting the Southern Pacific's progress at Yuma, Arizona. David Colton, a high-ranking associate of the Big Four, succumbed in October. As if these deaths were not enough to disrupt the affairs of the company, Leland Stanford fell seriously ill the following January and remained incapacitated through June 1879.[8] With Collis Huntington managing the company's financial and political affairs in the East, this left only Charles Crocker to lead the forces against adoption. In this he failed. On May 7, 1879, the constitution was ratified. California had a strong railroad commission, based on the assumption that the people of California would elect three incorruptible men. The three men who had composed the first advisory commission of 1876 had been honest, and California had elected many honorable governors in the past.[9] But past experience could not guarantee consistency. Once in operation, the constitutional reform which had been designed to eliminate the conflict of communities in regulatory rate-making would result in aiding the Big Four's negation of effective governmental controls for the rest of the century.

NOTES

1. Frank M. Fahey, "The Legislative Background of the California Constitutional Convention of 1878-1879" (Master's thesis, Stanford University, 1947), p. 90; *Sacramento Record-Union*, April 9, 1878, 2:1.
2. For a detailed analysis of deriving the numbers of influenced senators in California's legislative sessions of the seventies, see my "Local Interests and Railroad Regulation in Nineteenth Century California" (Doctoral dissertation, Stanford University, 1966), pp. 24-114.
3. *Debates and Proceedings of the Constitutional Convention of the State of California, Convened at the City of Sacramento, Saturday, September 28, 1878* (Sacramento, 1881), III, 1226, 1231; Mark Hopkins et al., *Letters from Mark Hopkins, Leland Stanford, Charles Crocker, Charles F. Crocker, and David D. Colton, to Collis P. Huntington, From August 27, 1869 to December 30, 1879* (New York, 1891), p. 215; Theodore H. Hittell, *History of California* (San Francisco, 1897), IV, 615; James Bryce, *The American Commonwealth* (New York, 1907), II, 436.
4. *Debates and Proceedings*, I, 557.

5. *Ibid.*, I, 487
6. In fact, rate regulation bills were repealed in Minnesota in 1875, in Wisconsin in 1876, and in Iowa in 1878.
7. *Debates and Proceedings,* I, 489, 564, 577, 604, 612; II, 1219; III, 1228, 1517-1518; George H. Miller, "The Granger Laws, A Study of the Origins of State Railway Control in the Upper Mississippi Valley" (Doctoral dissertation, University of Michigan, 1951), pp. 177-178, 187, 318-319, 320.
8. *Sacramento Record-Union,* Mar. 30, 1878, 3:3; Oct. 11, 1878, 2:3; Mark Hopkins et al., *Letters,* pp. 246-295.
9. *Debates and Proceedings,* I, 483, 526, 588.

PART
FIVE

Change Without Control

THE CURSE OF CALIFORNIA.

12

Regulating the Regulators

T HE English commentator on American life, James Bryce, visited California in the early 1880's and interviewed several of the surviving members of the Big Four. He asked them why their attorneys were not more actively petitioning the U.S. Supreme Court to accept an interpretation of the federal constitution's 14th Amendment which could void all unwanted state regulations. "The answer," he wrote years later, "was that they had considered this course, but had concluded that it was cheaper to capture a majority of the [Railroad] Commission."[1]

The first Railroad Commission under the new constitution was elected on September 3, 1879. Joseph S. Cone, a Republican and close friend of Leland Stanford, won his northern California district because of a split of the Democratic party into rival groups supporting "straight" and Workingmen's candidates. George Stoneman, a member of the old three-man commission created in 1876, was elected from southern California. Charles Beerstecher, a radical Workingmen's delegate to the constitutional convention, was chosen to represent San Francisco. Early in the first commission's sessions, Stoneman proposed that a maximum of five cents per ton mile be instituted for freight charges, a reform that would princi-

VOL. 7.   No 258.

The Wasp

SAN FRANCISCO, JULY 8TH 1881,

ENTERED AT THE POST OFFICE AT SAN FRANCISCO CAL AND ADMITTED FOR TRANSMISSION THROUGH THE MAILS AT SECOND CLASS RATES

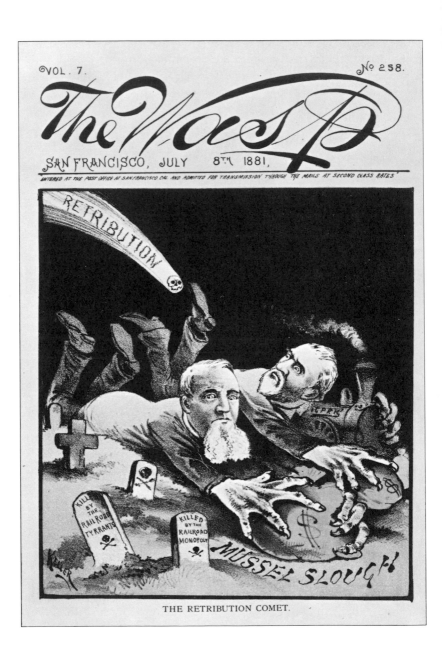

THE RETRIBUTION COMET.

pally help his southern California constituents who suffered from some of the highest rates in the state. But both Cone and Beerstecher vetoed the plan, surprising those who thought that the Workingmen's commissioner would vote for any proposal to lower rates. Beerstecher easily made the transition from sand-lot agitator to pro-railroad commissioner. "If companies can't make expenses, they have to cut down the number of their employees," he noted in justifying his switch. Later he was charged with selling out to the railroad because he feared that Stoneman might succumb to temptation, leaving him the sole anti-monopoly member of the commission, alone and poor.[2]

Only several reductions in rates were made by the first commission, and most of those benefited in minor ways the northern California constituents of Commissioner Cone. The local concentration of these reductions was all too apparent to George Stoneman.[3] On all crucial matters, the majority of the railroad commission carefully worked to protect the interests of Stanford and his associates. For instance, the new constitution prohibited *all* discrimination between places, which if literally enforced would have caused a drastic revision in the railroad companies' rate structures. However, the majority of the commission interpreted the prohibition out of existence:

> Were this Board to attempt the enforcement literally of this portion of the organic law, it would, first of all, be necessary to divest itself of that power of discrimination which our respective constituencies believed we possessed, when they elected us to the important positions of Railroad Commissioners. The judicial character with which the organic law has invested our office, has enabled us to exercise a judicious distinction, however, between 'just and unjust' discrimination.[4]

While the commission was emasculating the constitutional provisions by interpretation and administration, a new anti-railroad ferment was brewing. It was the result both of the pro-railroad commission and the Mussel Slough massacre of 1880, an incident climaxing a land titles dispute between the Southern Pacific and settlers in present-day Kings County. During a gun battle between representatives of the railroad and homesteaders at Mussel Slough, seven were killed in an episode symbolic of the rapacious "octo-

175

Joseph S. Cone, a friend of Leland Stanford representing northern California on the first Railroad Commission, succeeded in dominating that body to the chagrin of reformers in the State. — WRIGHTWOOD COLLECTION

pus." The Democrats capitalized on the angry expression of public opinion by framing a strong anti-railroad plank in their party platform of 1882. They nominated George Stoneman for governor, and on the surface it appeared that the Democratic party would inaugurate a new era of reform once in power. But behind the scenes, Stanford secured the Democratic nomination of two men he favored for railroad commissioners.[5]

Stoneman and the three Democratic nominees for the Railroad Commission were elected in 1882. But it soon became apparent that the railroad again controlled two of the three commissioners. This fact, added to the railroad's refusal to pay the taxes assessed by the State Board of Equalization, resulted in an outcry for severe action. And so in 1884, Governor Stoneman called the legislature into extra session to work solely on matters relating to railroad regulation and railroad taxation. Of the many bills and constitutional amendments introduced in 1884, the Barry bill particularly drew public attention. Submitted by a San Francisco assemblyman, it was designed to end the infectious special contract system, inaugurated by the Central Pacific in 1878 to eliminate all seagoing competition. By doubling its transcontinental rates and granting generous rebates to those shippers who would contract to send *all* of their freight by rail, the Central Pacific had succeeded in further perfecting its monopoly.[6]

In the legislature, the Central Pacific made threats and promises to line up specific localities against the Barry bill. Again it argued that the railroads could not afford to build into areas lacking railroad facilities unless they practiced certain discriminations, which would be outlawed by the bill. Charles Crocker informed the inhabitants of Placerville not to expect construction on the long-delayed extension from Shingle Springs to their town as long as anti-railroad agitation continued.[7] Henry Vrooman, who would become one of the original trustees of Stanford University the following year, spoke before the state senate in 1884 asking:

> What ought to be the position of the Senators from Plumas, Lake, Del Norte, Trinity, Mendocino, Calaveras, Mariposa, Ventura, and other counties which have not yet been brought into railroad communication with the rest of the State? . . . If an impetus can again be given to railroad construction in this State, there is a prospect for growth and prosperity in these counties, which will be impossible under legislation of the kind now under consideration — that this result will follow is evidenced by the experience in other States.[8]

However, the argument was not as effective as in times past, for by the 1880's fewer California counties lacked railroads. During the seventies, local desires and railroad influence had played relatively equal roles in defeating regulation measures in the senate. Corrupt tactics came more into play in the 1880's and 1890's. Following 1879, the legislature had a continuing popular mandate to enact legislation to enforce the new constitutional provisions, such as the prohibition of *all* discrimination in railroad matters. In order to insure against supplementary legislation like the Barry bill, Stanford's political machine found it necessary to invest more time and money in the legislature than ever before.[9]

Characteristically, the Barry bill was killed in the senate, where railroad politicos repeatedly stripped important sections from the measure until it was nothing but an empty shell. The story behind the mutilation of the bill in the senate focuses on the figure of Christopher A. Buckley, who ultimately reigned as the political boss of San Francisco for almost a decade. Beginning his political career in the early 1880's, he was able to build a strong Democratic party machine upon the ruins of the short-lived Workingmen's

First as Railroad Commissioner, then as Governor, Stoneman played an important but ineffectual role in California's railroad affairs during the 1880's.— BANCROFT LIBRARY

party. By the time of the extra session of 1884, he was a political force to be reckoned with in state politics, controlling most of the San Francisco delegation in the senate. Secretly planning to frighten the railroad into doing business with them, Buckley's men had originally persuaded Governor Stoneman to call the extra session. The naive governor had thought that he could depend on his Democratic majority in the senate, but the defeat of the Barry bill proved him wrong. Buckley's votes were sold. Nine of the ten Democratic senators from San Francisco voted with the railroad politicos.[10] Four or five additional votes against the bill were motivated by local considerations. The remaining handful of anti-Barry bill votes came from Stanford's regular retainers.

Compared with previous sessions, the Central Pacific spent great sums in achieving its ends in 1884. The United States Pacific Railway Commission, which investigated the company later in the decade, produced evidence indicating that the company probably spent more than $600,000 in influencing legislation that year. Because of the decline of local objections to regulation, more senators had to be bribed than ever before. And since the session was called to deal solely with railroad matters, numerous bills and constitutional amendments dealing with regulation and taxation had to be defeated. For example, one constitutional amendment proposed to have the railroad commissioners elected from the state at large instead of by district. The Central Pacific's tactic of concentrating its voting power in one or two districts had proved too effective. Another proposed to eliminate the railroad commission and put a rigid maximum rate schedule into the constitution itself. Both amendments, like all others inimical to the railroad's interests, were easily defeated because only one-third of the 40-member senate was needed to block changes to the constitution.[11]

Legislation to enforce the new constitution's taxation provisions was also odious to the Central Pacific. Always reluctant to pay taxes, the company was in court challenging the taxation sections of the state constitution while the reformers of 1884 introduced legislation to force the company to pay $2,500,000 in back taxes.[12] These bills met the same fate as the Barry bill. Meanwhile, the company's agents were also dispensing money in Kentucky, getting its legislature to approve the liberal charter of the "Southern Pacific Company," a new holding company for all the lines controlled by Stanford and his associates.* The purpose of this creation was to avoid certain California laws and force all suits originating in California to be heard in the federal courts.[13] Over all, the middle eighties proved to be expensive years for the Southern Pacific's political machine. Railroad commissions and legislatures had been regulated to insure the company control of events that could affect it. But as the Southern Pacific's directors would soon discover, such control was not to be had.

*Henceforth, even the parent Central Pacific would be known as the "Southern Pacific."

NOTES

1. James Bryce, *The American Commonwealth* (New York, 1907), II, 442.
2. *Report of the Committee on Corporations of the Assembly of California, Twenty-Fifth Session, 1883* (Sacramento, 1883), pp. 35, 53; *Sacramento Record-Union*, Sept. 27, 1879, 1:3; *San Francisco Bulletin*, May 15, 1880 (found in Stuart Daggett's California Notes [Bancroft Library, University of California, Berkeley], packet 76).
3. *Report of the Committee on Corporations, 1883*, p. 10.
4. California Railroad Commission, *Third-Annual Report of the Board of Railroad Commissioners* (Sacramento, 1882), p. 78.
5. *The Struggle of the Mussel Slough Settlers for their Homes! An Appeal to the People* (Visalia, 1880), pp. 1-32; *San Francisco Bulletin*, April 25, 1884, 2:3; Alexander Callow, Jr., "San Francisco's Blind Boss," *Pacific Historical Review*, XXV (1956), 272-273.
6. S. E. Moffett, "The Railroad Commission of California, A Study in Irresponsible Government," *Annals of the American Academy of Political and Social Science*, VI (1895), 112; John T. Doyle, *Railroad Rates and Transportation Overland. In a Letter (March 25, 1881) to a Member of Congress* (San Francisco, 1893), pp. 1-7; Julius Grodinsky, *Transcontinental Railway Strategy, 1869-1893: A Study of Businessmen* (Philadelphia, 1962), p. 71; *San Francisco Chronicle*, Aug. 10, 1878, 2:8; May 1, 1879, 4:1-2.
7. *Placerville Democrat*, Mar. 3, 1883 (found in Stuart Daggett's California Railroad Notes, packet 78).
8. Henry Vrooman, "Address on Railroads, Prepared for Delivery Before the California State Senate, Extra Session of 1884" (Typed copy at Timothy Hopkins Library, Stanford, California.), pp. 112-113.
9. John P. Irish, "California and the Railroad," *Overland Monthly*, XXV (1895), 675-681.
10. *San Francisco Bulletin*, May 1, 1884, 3:6; Callow, "Blind Boss," pp. 264, 274; *The Journal of the Senate During the Twenty-Fifth (Extra) Session of the Legislature of the State of California. 1884* (Sacramento, 1884), p. 74.
11. Charles Edward Russell, "Scientific Corruption of Politics," *Hampton's Magazine*, XXIV (1910), 853-854; *Journal of Senate, Extra Session, 1884*, p. 8; *San Francisco Bulletin*, April 5, 1884, 3:6.
12. *San Francisco Bulletin*, Oct. 8, 1892, 1:4; Gerald Nash, *State Government and Economic Development, A History of Administrative Policies in California, 1849-1933* (Berkeley, 1964), pp. 173-175.
13. California Railroad Commission, *Sixth Annual Report of the Board of Railroad Commissioners of the State of California, for the Year Ending December 31, 1885* (Sacramento, 1886), pp. 33-34; Neill C. Wilson and Frank J. Taylor, *Southern Pacific, The Roaring Story of a Fighting Railroad* (New York, 1952), p. 102; H. Brett Melendy and Benjamin F. Gilbert, *The Governors of California, Peter H. Burnett to Edmund G. Brown* (Georgetown, Calif., 1965), p. 250.

13

San Diego and the Santa Fe

ESPITE its success in the extra session of 1884, the Southern Pacific was simultaneously besieged with foreboding events outside the legislative halls. Rival transcontinental lines were invading its geographic area of control. Sadly for the Southern Pacific's directors, political control would be virtually worthless if the rumored profit-eroding rate wars occurred. As long as they possessed the *only* southern transcontinental railroad, they were capable of winning a rate war with any or all competitors situated on more difficult northern routes. Consequently, the Southern Pacific's profits depended upon blocking the completion of a rival southern transcontinental line. To fail to do so would invite disaster.

Throughout the 1870's, San Diego had worked for the completion of a rival southern road, but with the failure of Tom Scott the town had sought an accommodation with the hated Southern Pacific. Frank and Warren Kimball, developers owning much of the land immediately south of San Diego, had written Charles Crocker early in 1879 to encourage a Southern Pacific connection for the San Diego area. Crocker replied that if the "hoodlum constitution" of 1878 were ratified by the electorate in May, he and his

With his brother Warren, Frank Kimball who is pictured above, revived San Diego's railroad aspirations in the 1880's by inducing the Atchison, Topeka & Santa Fe Railway to extend its lines to southern California. (BELOW) San Diego, as it appeared in 1885. — BOTH WRIGHTWOOD COLLECTION

associates would "not want to build any more railroads in California." Nevertheless, the constitution was ratified, three-fourths of San Diego supporting the verdict. "They are as rabid down there as they can be," Crocker wrote to Huntington. The Southern Pacific would not come to San Diego. Undeterred, the Kimball brothers then contacted other railroad magnates, Commodore Vanderbilt and Jay Gould among them. Gould was unusually frank. "I don't build railroads, I buy them," he wrote the Kimballs. Finally, in the fall of 1879, they succeeded in persuading the Atchison, Topeka and Santa Fe Railroad to terminate in San Diego, in exchange for a modest financial subsidy and a generous grant of land. For its part, the Santa Fe agreed to build along a direct route from San Diego to Yuma.[1]

Hearing of San Diego's good fortune, a San Bernardino citizens' committee made strenuous efforts to alter the Santa Fe's route into California. The San Diego to Yuma survey would leave San Bernardino far off the main line, whereas a more northerly route from Needles through the Cajon Pass and on to San Diego would pass through their town. Despite San Diego's efforts to defeat the San Bernardino idea, the railroad company found it irresistible, for the new route would serve a larger population and result in greater profits. Concurrently with these events, the Santa Fe acquired half interest in the Atlantic and Pacific, a railroad company with a large federal land grant dating back to 1866. The Atlantic and Pacific, as the Pacific link of the Santa Fe, would enter California at Needles near the 35th parallel. These aggreements nullified the pact between the Santa Fe and San Diego.[2]

After all of their thwarted attempts, San Diegans were willing to settle for almost any guarantee of a rail connection which would make their town a transcontinental terminus. So a new arrangement between San Diego and the Santa Fe was consummated. A corporation called the California Southern would build northward from San Diego toward San Bernardino, with the intention of meeting the Atlantic and Pacific. Chartered in October 1880, the California Southern commenced construction the following June among the cheers of San Diegans. But not all southern Californians celebrated the event. Angelinos were noticably glum, fearing that completion of this second transcontinental line might enable San

The Atlantic & Pacific, temporarily delayed at Needles, successfully thrust deep into southern California in 1884. This scene shows, the 12-stall roundhouse and machine shop on the California side of the Colorado River. — SANTA FE RAILWAY COLLECTION

Diego to bypass Los Angeles as the chief city of southern California. In fact, they even went so far as to encourage Congress to strip the Atlantic and Pacific of part of its old land grant, a move which almost succeeded four years later.[3]

Meanwhile, the directors of the Southern Pacific were engaged in secret maneuvers to maintain their hegemony. By strategic purchases of stock in early 1882, Huntington and his temporary ally Jay Gould acquired control of the St. Louis and San Francisco Railroad, which like the Santa Fe held half interest in the westward building Atlantic and Pacific. By this coup, Huntington forced the Atlantic and Pacific to stop at Needles. There, the Santa Fe reluctantly agreed, the Atlantic and Pacific would connect with a Southern Pacific branch from Mojave. By August 1883 the connection was made, and Santa Fe cars entered California over track controlled by the Southern Pacific. This arrangement was most unsatisfactory for the Santa Fe, because the Southern Pacific channeled the trade of California over its own line via Yuma by means of discriminatory practices on its track west of Needles. With the prospects of the Santa Fe dimming, the railroad outlook was "gloomy for San Bernardino, and black — dead black — for San Diego." "We'll buy the Santa Fe yet for the cost of its rails," exulted a Southern Pacific agent in Colton. Ultimate victory appeared always to belong to the California monopoly.[4]

By the fall of 1884, the Santa Fe gained an unobstructed entrance into southern California, forcing the Southern Pacific to sell its track from Needles to Mojave by threatening to inaugurate ruinous transcontinental competition to Guaymas over its Sonora Railway line in Mexico. Huntington was beaten.[5] With the Cali-

Gould and Huntington joined forces to stall briefly the expansion of the Atlantic & Pacific. They were outsmarted by the Santa Fe Railway. — DONALD DUKE COLLECTION

185

The tracks of the California Southern passed through Temecula Canyon which the railroad company later learned from bitter experience was prone to flash flooding. — TITLE INSURANCE & TRUST CO. — SAN DIEGO

San Diego's harbor, second only to San Francisco, destined San Diego as the railroad center of southern California — or so thought San Diego's 19th-century boosters. The scene above shows No. 3, a four-wheel switcher at the foot of Front Street on the bay in 1882. — TITLE INSURANCE & TRUST CO. — SAN DIEGO (BELOW) By-passed by the Southern Pacific in its march through southern California in 1876, San Bernardinians eagerly greeted the California Southern's first train in 1883. — GERALD M. BEST COLLECTION

People from the East were lured to California by falling transcontinental passenger rates during the mid-1880's. In this scene boomers gathered for a portrait along the lines of the Southern Pacific. — DONALD DUKE COLLECTION

fornia Southern at San Bernardino and the Santa Fe controlling track 50 miles to the north, construction began in Cajon Pass to bridge the gap. A year later the work was completed; by November 1885, the Santa Fe had a rival southern transcontinental line, terminating in San Diego. The long-awaited event was celebrated in San Diego with "many speeches marked with flights of imagination concerning the tremendous benefits which were to accrue to the city." San Bernardino likewise rejoiced with fireworks, speeches, brass bands, and a barbeque. San Bernardino's newspapers commemorated the affair as "this important event, the most important in our history." "San Bernardino . . . will no longer be ignored as heretofore, but will take her proper place as the second city of southern California," concluded one editorial.[6]

The cheering had scarcely stopped, when the long-expected transcontinental rate war erupted. The completion of other transcontinental lines — the Northern Pacific to Portland in 1883 and an extension of the Union Pacific to the same city in the following year — had caused some earlier uneasiness in rates and periodic stabilizing agreements. However, all such arrangements were

188

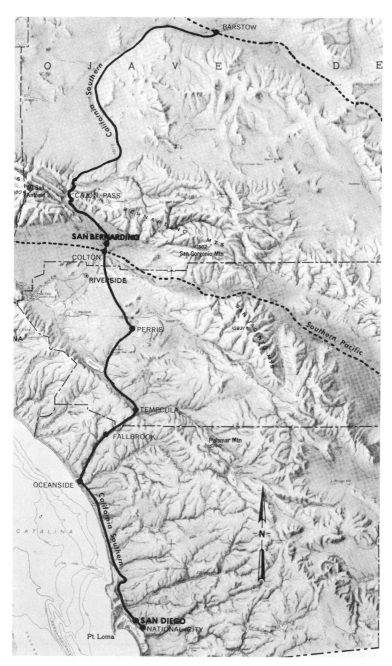

The Route of the California Southern — 1885

shattered by the completion of the second southern transcontinental road. As a prerequisite to any new agreement, the Santa Fe demanded 50 percent of the business of southern California and 27 percent of northern California's trade. The Southern Pacific refused to meet these conditions, and the rate slashing began. Late in 1885, before the rate war fully commenced, a ticket between Kansas City and Los Angeles sold for $70. Early the following year, rates began dropping rapidly. By March 6, as one story goes, the charge was one dollar. This anecdote has no basis in fact, but its frequent use has served to dramatize the real cutthroat quality of this competition among giants. Low transcontinental rates continued through 1886, not merely to Los Angeles but to San Francisco and other Pacific coast communities as well.[7]

Few Californians could complain of railroad tyranny during this period.[8] Inexpensive tickets spelled increased immigration, which in turn encouraged a real estate boom in southern California and general prosperity in the state at large. Even reformers muffled their criticism. Stephen Mallory White, who had joined the anti-railroad movement of the early eighties and who would later win fame for his attacks on the Southern Pacific in the 1890's,

By the late 1880's, Redondo was established as one of the Santa Fe's Pacific ports. This view shows the long wharf where a Pacific Coast Steamship Co. vessel is docked. Redondo held commercial importance as a lumber and merchandise port. — R. P. MIDDLEBROOK

Long ignored by the Southern Pacific, Santa Barbara finally welcomed its first train on August 18, 1887. Local citizens were out to celebrate the event. — DONALD DUKE COLLECTION

mirrored the changing public mood. During the latter half of the 1880's, White worked as a Southern Pacific attorney at a time when he was also a member of the California state senate. By 1887, many Californians, especially those in the southern part of the State, could agree with a statement made by John C. Stubbs, General Traffic Manager of the Southern Pacific: "The interests of the railroad companies and the communities they serve are identical."[9]

Nevertheless, some southern California localities failed to achieve their total expectations during the latter half of the decade. Ballona (today Playa del Rey) proclaimed herself "the future harbor of southern California," "the ocean terminus of the Atchison and Santa Fe system," only to lose the latter title to Redondo Beach in 1887. Santa Barbara, after several decades of anxious waiting, was linked with Los Angeles by the Southern Pacific in 1887. However, construction north of Santa Barbara ended, thus depriving the community of a connection with San Francisco until 1901. But the greatest disappointment of that era belonged to San

By 1899, the Santa Fe Railway system in southern California was more developed than it was in 1885. Note the abandonment of the old line of the California Southern through Temecula Canyon as well as the addition of a new coastal line to San Diego.

By 1887, when this photograph was made of the Santa Fe's shop facilities at National City, the major repair center had moved to San Bernardino. — DONALD DUKE COLLECTION

Diego, for in 1887 the Santa Fe bought and built its way from San Bernardino into Los Angeles and there commenced to establish its principal southern California terminus.[10]

During the early eighties, San Diegans had mocked the possibility that they would someday be spurned by the Santa Fe for Los Angeles. A San Diego historian had ridiculed the harbor facilities at San Pedro/Wilmington in 1883: "There are several . . . places above San Diego that are called harbors, just as every third-grade country school teacher in California is a 'professor.'" This principal port of Los Angeles, concluded the historian, would never rival San Diego, "by any stretch either of fancy or government funds." But the rhetoric of local jealousies did not sweep aside the harsh commercial realities of transcontinental competition. Los Angeles was much larger than its southern rival, thus offering more business to the Santa Fe. Repeated washouts of the California Southern's track between San Bernardino and San Diego further encouraged the Santa Fe to rely on the ports of Los Angeles as its principal outlets to the sea. Finally, the Santa Fe's principal machine shops and general offices were moved from National City, near San Diego, to San Bernardino and Los Angeles, respectively. Only a residue

193

of bitter memories was left, of broken promises by a railroad company once seen as the harbinger of San Diego's greatness.[11]

NOTES

1. Mark Hopkins et al., *Letters from Mark Hopkins, Leland Stanford, Charles Crocker, Charles F. Crocker, and David D. Colton, to Collis P. Huntington, From August 27, 1869 to December 30, 1879* (New York, 1891), pp. 272, 287-288, 289, 294; Lewis B. Lesley, "The Struggle of San Diego for a Southern Transcontinental Railroad Connection, 1854-1891" (Doctoral dissertation, University of California, Berkeley, 1933), p. 254; Glenn S. Dumke, *The Boom of the Eighties in Southern California* (San Marino, Calif., 1944), pp. 136-137.
2. Franklyn Hoyt, "Railroad Development in Southern California, 1868 to 1900" (Doctoral dissertation, University of Southern California, 1951), p. 254; Luther A. Ingersoll, *Ingersoll's Century Annals of San Bernardino County, 1769 to 1904* (Los Angeles, 1904), pp. 257-258.
3. William S. Greever, *Arid Domain, The Santa Fe Railway and Its Western Land Grant* (Stanford, 1954), pp. 34-35; Hoyt, "Railroad Development," pp. 256, 295-296; Lesley, "The Struggle of San Diego," p. 264.
4. Dumke, *The Boom of the Eighties*, pp. 136-137; F. E. Prendergast, "Transcontinental Railways," *Harper's Magazine*, LXVII (1883), 940-941; Glenn Bradley, *The Story of the Santa Fe* (Boston, 1920), p. 222; Julius Grodinsky, *Transcontinental Railway Strategy, 1869-1893* (Philadelphia, 1962), p. 217; Ingersoll, *San Bernardino County*, p. 261; James Marshall, *Santa Fe, The Railroad that Built an Empire* (New York, 1945), pp. 186-187; H. Craig Miner *The St. Louis-San Francisco Transcontinental Railroad, The Thirty-Fifth Parallel Project, 1853-1890* (Lawrence, Kansas, 1972), pp. 130-131.
5. Marshall, *Santa Fe*, p. 172; Lawrence Leslie Waters, *Steel Trails to Santa Fe* (Lawrence, Kan., 1950), pp. 61-62; Prendergast, "Transcontinental Railways," 940-941; Glenn Chesney Quiett, *They Built the West, An Epic of Rails and Cities* (New York, 1934), p. 274; Hoyt, "Railroad Development," p. 276; Lewis B. Lesley, "The Entrance of the Santa Fe Railroad into California," *Pacific Historical Review*, VIII (1939), 92-95.
6. Donald Duke and Stan Kistler, *Santa Fe, Steel Rails Through California* (San Marino, Calif., 1963), pp. 26-29; Lesley, "The Entrance of the Santa Fe," p. 96; Hoyt, "Railroad Development, p. 282; *San Bernardino Times*, Nov. 14, 1885, quoted in Ingersoll, *San Bernardino County*, p. 262.
7. Grodinsky, *Transcontinental Railway Strategy*, pp. 258-261, 319; Quiett, *They Built the West*, p. 275; J. Netz, "The Great Los Angeles Real Estate Boom of 1887," *Historical Society of Southern California, Annual Publications*, X (1915), 56; Dumke, *The Boom of the Eighties*, pp. 24-25; Donald Duke, publisher of Golden West Books, in researching his *Santa Fe, Steel Rails Through California*, examined existing passenger tariffs from the period and found no documentation to support the well-known tale of the dollar fare.
8. Leland Stanford's election to the United States Senate and a proposed state constitutional amendment to ease the Southern Pacific's tax burden, both in 1885, were widely criticized. But with the rate war, other issues besides those concerning railroads came to dominate California politics. (See William C. Fankhauser's *A Financial History of California Public Revenues, Debts, and Expenditures* [Berkeley, 1913], pp. 282-283). For example, the irrigation issue prompted Governor Stoneman to call a second special session of the legislature

in 1886. (Theodore H. Hittell, *History of California* [San Francisco, 1898], IV, 695).

9. Edith Dobie, *The Political Career of Stephen Mallory White, A Study of Party Activities Under the Convention System* (Stanford, Calif., 1927), pp. 100-102; *Testimony Taken by the United States Pacific Railway Commission, Appointed Under the Act of Congress Approved March 3, 1887, Entitled 'An Act Authorizing an Investigation of the Books, Accounts, and Methods of Railroads Which Have Received Aid from the United States, and For Other Purposes'* (Washington, 1887), VI, 3332; Dumke, *The Boom of the Eighties,* p. 275.

10. Dumke, *The Boom of the Eighties,* pp. 64-65, 130; Hoyt, "Railroad Development," pp. 119-120, 310-313; James M. Guinn, *Historical and Biographical Record of Southern California, From Its Earliest Settlement to the Opening Year of the Twentieth Century* (Chicago, 1902), p. 171.

11. Wallace W. Elliot, *History of San Bernardino and San Diego Counties, California, 1883* (Riverside, Calif., 1965, reprint), p. 161; Ingersoll, *San Bernardino County,* pp. 262-266; Lesley, "The Struggle of San Diego," pp. 321-330.

The open meadow and wooden fenced right of way in this pastoral scene of 1884 hardly resembles today's Burlingame. Trains such as this, symbolized Southern Pacific's dominance of western commerce. — SOUTHERN PACIFIC COLLECTION

14

San Francisco's Reaction

THROUGHOUT the 1870's, the Big Four had discriminated in favor of San Francisco in order to maximize long-haul profits. But when the Santa Fe began to unload Chicago merchandise in Arizona, the Southern Pacific changed its policy toward the bay city. And the Big Four's charges on freight shipped from Chicago to Arizona (by way of the San Joaquin Valley) dropped below those on merchandize shipped directly from San Francisco. "Is this the object for which the Southern Pacific Railroad was built?" complained the *San Francisco Chronicle*. "Did not the railroad magnates allege, long before it ever reached Yuma, that if San Francisco men controlled the railroads to Arizona we should also control the trade of that region?" Slowly and painfully, bay city merchants came to understand a rule of railroad economics later articulated by historian Edward C. Kirkland: "Railroads sought maximum profits, not the urban hegemony of the cities that promoted them." The company's goal of maximizing profits had remained constant throughout, but the new pressures of railroad competition brought about a change in means.[1]

The commencement of transcontinental railroad competition inevitably led to the dismemberment of San Francisco's old commercial empire. Portland and Los Angeles increasingly received trade that had traditionally gone to San Francisco. A change in California agriculture also contributed to San Francisco's plight. Increasingly, citrus fruits and early garden crops were replacing grains as California's primary exports. Unlike wheat, which left the state by sea, oranges and perishable vegetables had to be shipped by rail to prevent spoilage. The eastern connections of the Southern Pacific agreed to carry this produce at relatively low rates but only in exchange for agreements which allowed eastern merchants to increase their penetration of San Francisco's commercial territory.[2]

Nevertheless, the rate war of the eighties brought temporary benefits to the bay city which helped lessen the pain of its commercial adjustment. For one, the special contract system, which had diminished the flow of sea traffic through the Golden Gate without any compensations to the city, was an early casualty of the transcontinental competition. San Francisco's interior trade also prospered. "The commerce diverted from San Francisco by the construction of railways to terminals north and south of us, has been fully replaced by an increased trade in the territory tributary to this city," noted the president of San Francisco's Chamber of Commerce in 1883.[3]

These good times were only temporary. San Francisco's merchants began to feel the effects of their shrunken trading empire when the transcontinental pooling agreements were restored at the close of the decade, but they did not surrender to the new order without a struggle. One merchant was especially optimistic that San Francisco's dominance of western commerce could be revived. He chartered a British ship to carry a cargo of goods from New York to Antwerp and thence to San Francisco, the "broken voyage" being necessitated by American coastal shipping laws. The purpose of this experiment was to see how much of a saving could be made over the charges of American shipping, thought to be controlled by the transcontinental railroads. When the ship arrived in San Francisco in October 1891, the news spread that the experimenting merchant had made a considerable saving. San Francisco's merchants then organized their own steamship company to be operated in the interests of San Francisco commerce. This competition broke the transcontinental pool in 1892, and a new rate war was inaugurated.[4]

Achieving low transcontinental rates to San Francisco was only the first step in reviving the city's commercial prominence. Isaac Upham, a San Francisco merchant leading the uprising against the railroad, hinted at the next move: "Local railroad rates are even more important to San Francisco merchants than the sea freights, for if they cannot distribute to the interior it does them little good to heap their warehouses with goods brought by the ships."[5] Faced with a railroad commission unwilling to reduce interior rates, San Francisco's merchants spearheaded a drive in 1893 to abolish the commission. A constitutional amendment was drafted by the Traffic Association of California, a San Francisco merchants' organization, and was submitted to the legislature in 1893 by a San Francisco senator. Including a stringent maximum rate schedule within its provisions, the amendment also authorized a downward revision of rates at the state legislature's discretion. Only roads earning more than $4,000 per mile annually would be so regulated.[6]

Testifying before the legislative committee reviewing the amendment, Joseph S. Leeds, a leader of the San Francisco merchants, claimed that the amendment's rate schedule would enable the Southern Pacific to make a reasonable profit. But what about California's many short railroad lines? As the evidence was amassed it became apparent, even to Leeds, that a number of short lines could not make a reasonable profit under the amendment. If such were the case, it was argued, the proposed amendment would violate the due process clause of the federal constitution's 14th Amendment. "It is badly drawn," said one observer of the measure. "It was aimed at the Southern Pacific Company, but it is like the blunderbuss loaded with scrap iron; it shoots everybody· in the neighborhood." Legislators from communities served by these short lines were convinced that the San Francisco merchants were solely interested in reducing their own rates over the Southern Pacific. The San Franciscans faced a dilemma. If the amendment were redrawn to regulate only the major railroads in the State, it would most probably be ruled unconstitutional on the grounds of violating the equal protection clause of the same 14th Amendment. "You can't harm us much," a Southern Pacific agent cockily told the legislative committee reviewing the amendment:

> because we are protected by the Constitution; pass it and you can't enforce it; it would become to us a matter of indifference, but it is a question of the Legislature and of this committee, because under the Fourteenth Amendment of the Constitution of the United States, corporations are persons, and no State can deny to any person within its limits the equal protection of the law, and that is the declaration of the Fourteenth Amendment to the Constitution.[7]

Whatever form the amendment took, it seemed that the courts were likely to declare it unconstitutional.[8]

The measure failed in the assembly by two votes to gain the necessary two-thirds support required for a constitutional amendment. Of the 22 votes against the amendment, roughly half had the warm support of their constituencies. Most of the representatives from southern California opposed the measure for local reasons. San Luis Obispo and Santa Barbara were still awaiting the completion of the Southern Pacific's coast line route. The inhabitants of the Los Angeles basin were looking forward to a railroad to connect their community directly with Utah, and a promoter of this road had warned that the amendment would prevent its construction. Angelinos were quarreling with the Southern Pacific at this time over the prospective site for a federally financed harbor for their city, but they did not let their feelings blind them into supporting the amendment which had nothing to do with the harbor and which was inimical to the interests of Los Angeles. Southern California orange growers saw no benefit in lowering *intrastate* rates. They also feared that the Southern Pacific might respond to the passage of the amendment by raising its *interstate* rates, the levels of which determined the orange growers' profits. And finally, the Los Angeles/San Diego area of the state was a commercial rival of San Francisco and viewed with suspicion any bill supported so unanimously by San Franciscans. Other scattered counties in the state were against the amendment because it would prevent railroads from undertaking desired construction or would kill already existent short lines.[9] In fact, even several of the session's Populist assemblymen, mindful of the local interests of their constituents,

The Traffic Association broadcast the news that the Bay Area
(broadly interpreted as *California* in the poster) was being
victimized. Snakes were used to symbolize the Southern Pacific.
— WRIGHTWOOD COLLECTION

voted against the amendment. The remainder of those opposing
the measure did so either because of an affinity for the Southern
Pacific or because they simply recognized the weaknesses of the
proposal.

After the defeat of the amendment, San Franciscans began
thinking of new ways to lower their shipping costs within California. "We are fast losing ground," Isaac Upham told his compatriots
in October 1894, "and unless something is done quickly, the trade
of the [San Joaquin] Valley will be lost to San Francisco. Goods
from here have even been shipped there via Los Angeles."[10] San

Joseph Leeds   **Isaac Upham**

Leeds and Upham led the Traffic Association of California, an
organization created in the 1890's to promote the railroad interests of the Bay Area. — BANCROFT LIBRARY

Franciscans discussed building their own railroad down the valley,
but few seemed willing to raise the capital necessary for the project.
Meanwhile, Kings County in the San Joaquin Valley began to press
for its construction. Late in November 1894, leading Kings County
citizens petitioned the Los Angeles Chamber of Commerce to build
a competing road north from Los Angeles to capture all of the
valley trade for that growing city. In a January meeting in the following year, the Los Angeles Chamber of Commerce discussed
the idea enthusiastically, giving the impression that it might fulfill
the dream of Kings County. News of this meeting drove San Francisco's merchants to action. They quickly organized under the
leadership of Claus Spreckels to build the long-debated railroad
down the valley.[11]

In selecting the exact route of the valley road, Spreckels was as
ruthless as the Big Four had ever been. Eager localities were told
that they would have to purchase substantial amounts of the new
company's stock and offer sufficient land and rights-of-way or be
bypassed. An article in the *San Francisco Examiner,* the leading
organ of the project, exhibited the raw flavor of such appeals to
local self-interest:

Claus Spreckles directed the fortunes of the San Francisco & San Joaquin Valley Railway. Of a wealthy family, Spreckles boasted that he had never failed at any major undertaking. — WRIGHTWOOD COLLECTION

As President Spreckels himself says, the route must depend largely upon what the different cities down the valley and along the peninsula may be inclined to do to insure that line shall not pass to the east of them. Stockton is to be the starting point and from there to the Stanislaus County line alone has the general course of the route been laid out. Just now it is known that Stockton will be the starting point with Bakersfield in all probability the ultimate objective point, provided that the latter city offers sufficient inducements. Not a single intermediate point on the road between the two cities has yet been fixed. It remains with the hundreds of small towns to decide what they will do to work out their own salvation.[12]

Construction of the line commenced from Stockton late in 1895. A year later Fresno had been reached, and on May 27, 1898, the road was completed to Bakersfield. But the fanfare was shortlived. Less than a year later, the valley road was sold to the Santa Fe, without the direct consent of most of those who had contributed money to the enterprise. Most San Franciscans were shocked by the transaction, for as historian Stuart Daggett later pointed out, "the argument that the construction of the San Francisco and San Joaquin Valley Railway would prevent the diversion of eastern freight from San Francisco to distributing centers of the South" could not easily "be reconciled with the sale of the railroad to a company which, like the Santa Fe, had a terminus in Los Angeles."[13] Spreckels could easily justify the sale in his own mind,

203

Completion of the San Francisco & San Joaquin Valley broke the Southern Pacific stronghold on the San Joaquin Valley. A momentous event was taking place in this scene, as the first train called the *Emancipator* made its way along the line between Stockton and Bakersfield on October 5, 1896. — SANTA FE RAILWAY

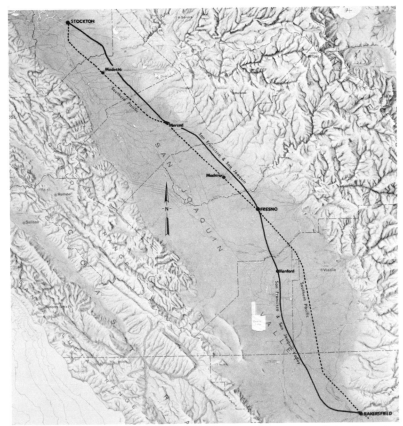

having assumed that San Francisco's merchants could take advantage of competition between the Southern Pacific and the Santa Fe. But this hope quickly died. The Southern Pacific, which had been forced by the competition of the valley road to lower its charges, joined with the Santa Fe in raising rates. The Southern Pacific and the Santa Fe had to violate the California constitution in making their new pooling agreement, for Section 20 of Article XII stipulated:

> Whenever a railroad corporation shall, for the purpose of competing with any other common carrier, lower its rates for transportation of passengers or freight from one point to another, such reduced rates shall not be again raised or increased from such standard without the consent of the governmental authority, in which shall be vested the power to regulate fares and freights.[14]

205

Interested parties sued the Southern Pacific for violating the constitutional provision. Litigation lasted until 1904 when Judge Frank Kerrigan of the Superior Court of San Francisco ruled in favor of the railroad company. The Southern Pacific, he reasoned, had not lowered its rates but had rather charged a lower rate for a new inferior service. When the company later seemingly raised its rates it was not violating the constitution but was merely abolishing the inferior service and the low rate that went with it. After this decision, appeal was made to the California Supreme Court. Here, in the Fresno Rate Case of 1904, the Southern Pacific won another victory but on different grounds than in the lower court decision. It was not the intent of the framers, the court said, "to punish a corporation for merely lowering its rates in self-defense to meet a lower rate inaugurated by a rival carrier."[15]

The San Francisco merchants had failed to secure lower California rates by building a competing road in the San Joaquin Valley. In addition, they lost simultaneously in attempting to change the character of the California Railroad Commission, which they had unsuccessfully tried to abolish in 1893. In 1894, a reformer was elected from San Francisco's railroad commissioner district with the energetic support of the Traffic Association. Another of the elected commissioners was pledged "to down the corporation." Those people desiring lower California freight rates believed that they had a reformer-dominated commission at last. Once in office the new commission failed to act. Only the San Francisco reformer remained true to his pledges. To soften growing cries for a reduction in rates, the Southern Pacific voluntarily lowered its grain rates in certain areas of the State. Then, in a surprise move, the commission unanimously decided to impose an additional reduction in grain rates. The San Francisco commissioner honestly supported the reduction. However, it is possible that the other two were directed to do so by the Southern Pacific, which wanted to bring a test case to the courts.[16]

The Southern Pacific immediately appealed to Judge Joseph McKenna of the United States Circuit Court for northern California. He responded by issuing a sweeping injunction, halting the commission's edict from going into effect. A trial then ensued in McKenna's court. The railroad's attorneys contended that the commission's rates would not provide the company with "just compensation" and therefore would violate the due process clause of the 14th Amendment. The attorneys for the commission rested their case on the California constitutional provision that rates set by the commission were to "be deemed *conclusively* just and reasonable." In 1896, McKenna, who would soon be promoted to the Supreme Court, decided in favor of the company. For many years thereafter, the California Railroad Commission would be generally regarded as a worthless appendage of state government.[17]

McKenna's decision symbolized the Southern Pacific's invincibility, a popular image increasingly becoming closer to caricature than true likeness. The California railroad company had been forced to share power with rival firms in order to keep temporary pooling agreements alive. It had also been unable to prevent the destructive rate wars of the 19th century's last two decades. An old order was passing for *both* San Francisco's merchants and the state's railroad leaders. Change appeared to be the only constant — change without control.

NOTES

1. *San Francisco Chronicle,* Aug. 25, 1879 (found in Bancroft Scraps [Bancroft Library, University of California, Berkeley], LXXX, 888); Edward C. Kirkland, *Men, Cities and Transportation, A Study in New England History, 1820-1900* (Cambridge, Mass., 1948), I, 528.
2. *San Francisco Bulletin,* Mar. 28, 1888, 2:1; *Sacramento Record-Union,* Oct. 26, 1891, 2:1; *Daily Alta California,* April 11, 1873, 2:1; *Testimony Taken by the United States Pacific Railway Commission, Appointed Under the Act of Congress Approved March 3, 1887, Entitled 'An Act Authorizing an Investigation of the Books, Accounts, and Methods of Railroads Which Have Received Aid From the United States, and For Other Purposes'* (Washington, 1887), V, 2807-2808.
3. San Francisco Chamber of Commerce, *Thirty-Fifth Annual Report of the Chamber of Commerce of San Francisco, Submitted to a Meeting Held Jan. 20, 1885* (San Francisco, 1885), p. 7; San Francisco Chamber of Commerce, *Thirty-Eighth Annual Report of the Chamber of Commerce of San Francisco, Submitted to a Meeting Held January 17, 1888* (San Francisco, 1888), n.p.
4. Wheeler Publishing Co., *The Valley Road, A History of the Traffic Association of California, The League of Progress, The North American Navigation Company, The Merchants Shipping Association and San Joaquin Valley Railway* (San Francisco, 1896), pp. 8-9, 60-61; Neill C. Wilson and Frank J. Taylor, *Southern Pacific, The Roaring Story of a Fighting Railroad* (New York, 1952), p. 118; Julius Grodinsky, *Transcontinental Railway Strategy, 1869-1893: A Study of Businessmen* (Philadelphia, 1962), p. 360; San Francisco Daily Morning Call Co., *Fettered Commerce, How the Pacific Mail and the Railroads Have Bled San Francisco* (San Francisco, 1892), p. 27.

5. Wheeler Publishing Co., *The Valley Road*, p. 61.
6. California Senate Committee on Constitutional Amendments, *Report of the Testimony and Proceedings Taken Before the Senate Committee on Constitutional Amendments, Relative to Senate Constitutional Amendment No. 8, Abrogating Provisions of Constitution as to Railroad Commission, and Placing Distance Tariff in Constitution* (Sacramento, 1893), p. ix.
7. *Ibid.*, pp. 2-3, 46, 123-124; *San Francisco Bulletin*, Feb. 1, 1893, 1:7; California Railroad Commission, *Annual Report, 1893-1894* (Sacramento, 1894), pp. 31-32; *San Francisco Examiner*, Jan. 30, 1893, 8:3-4.
8. The Southern Pacific had played a major role in pushing for the court's acceptance of this new interpretation of the 14th Amendment. In 1882, Roscoe Conkling, a member of the congressional committee that drafted the amendment in 1866 and a retainer of Huntington since 1868, testified before the Supreme Court in a case involving the Southern Pacific that the intent of the amendment's framers was to protect corporations as well as black and white unionists from state discrimination. [See: James F. Russell, "The Railroads in the 'Conspiracy Theory' of the Fourteenth Amendment," *Mississippi Valley Historical Review*, XLI (1955), 601-602; Collis P. Huntington, *Letters from Collis P. Huntington to Mark Hopkins, Leland Stanford, Charles Crocker, E. B. Crocker, Charles F. Crocker, and David D. Colton* (New York, 1892-1894), I, 280, 354]. Shortly thereafter, the court began to exhibit a growing acceptance of this doctrine. In an orbiter dictum in *Stone v. Farmers' Loan and Trust Company*, Chief Justice Waite stated: "Under pretense of regulating fares and freights, the State cannot require a railroad corporation to carry persons or property without reward; neither can it do that which in law amounts to a taking of private property without reward; neither can it do that which in law amounts to a taking of private property for public use without just compensation, or without due process of law." (See: *Stone v. Farmers' Loan and Trust Company*, 116 U.S. 307). A thorough development of this doctrine by the court would wait until the 1890's. [See: *Chicago, Milwaukee, and St. Paul Railway Co. v. Minnesota*, 134, U.S. 418; *Budd v. New York*, 143 U.S. 517; *Chicago and Grand Trunk Railroad v. Wellman*, 143 U.S. 339; *Reagan v. Farmers' Loan and Trust Company*, 154 U.S. 398; *Smyth v. Ames*, 169 U.S. 466. Also see: H. S. Smalley, "Railway Rate Control in its Legal Aspects," *American Economic Association Publication*, VII (1906), 365-366].
9. California Senate Committee on Constitutional Amendments, *Report*, pp. 45, 46-47, 62; *San Francisco Bulletin*, Mar. 3, 1893, 2:3; Stuart Daggett, *Chapters on the History of the Southern Pacific* (Berkeley, 1922), pp. 238-239.
10. Wheeler Publishing Co., *The Valley Road*, p. 74.
11. Eugene L. Menefee and Fred A. Dodge, *History of Tulare and Kings Counties, Calif.* (Los Angeles, 1913), pp. 202-207.
12. *San Francisco Examiner*, April 4, 1895, 9:1.
13. James Marshall, *Santa Fe, The Railroad that Built an Empire* (New York, 1945), p. 259; Daggett, *Southern Pacific*, p. 332.
14. *Debates and Proceedings of the Constitutional Convention of the State of California, Convened at the City of Sacramento, Saturday, September 28, 1878* (Sacramento, 1881), III, 1517-1518.
15. Charles Edward Russell, "The Remedy of the Law," *Hampton's Magazine*, XXV (1910), 219; C. P. Connolly, "Big Business and the Bench," *Everybody's Magazine*, XXVI (1912), 296-297; E. B. Edson et al., *Board of Railroad Commissioners of California, Appellants v. Southern Pacific Railroad Company, Respondents*, 144 California Reports 182; or 77 Pacific Reporter 894.

16. S. E. Moffett, "The Railroad Commission of California, A Study in Irresponsible Government," *Annals of the American Academy of Political and Social Science,* VI (1895), 115-116; Gerald Nash, "The Role of State Government in the Economy of California, 1849-1911" (Doctoral dissertation, University of California, Berkeley, 1957), p. 322.

17. "The Railroad Commission of California," *Transactions of the Commonwealth Club of California,* III (1908), 345; *Southern Pacific Co. v. Board of Railroad Commissioners of California et al.,* 78 Federal Reporter 236; "The Courts, the Plutocracy and the People," *Arena,* XXXVI (1906), 86; "Second Biennial Message of Governor George C. Pardee," *Appendix to Journals of Senate and Assembly, California, Thirty-Seventh Session — 1907* (Sacramento, 1907), I, 48-49.

The old Los Angeles Arcade Station of the Southern Pacific forms a scene for this 1891 portrait of No. 1364 and her proud crew. — DONALD DUKE COLLECTION

15

The Challenge of Despair

B Y the end of the century, disillusionment lived in the commercial circles of San Diego and San Francisco. The former town's businessmen had failed to direct the path of southern transcontinental railroad traffic to their desires, while San Francisco's merchants had failed in their numerous attempts to recreate old discriminations which had been enjoyed before transcontinental railroad competition. The San Franciscans had lost in their efforts to abolish and later reform the Railroad Commission and to control their own railroad down the San Joaquin Valley. Their steamship competition with the Pacific Mail Steamship Company had also died out in early 1896.[1] This general record of failure had early been predicted by the Southern Pacific's organ in Sacramento. Viewing the formation of the San Francisco merchants' organization that was to give shape to the spirit of revolt, the *Sacramento Record-Union* had proclaimed: "No convention, however numerously attended, to form traffic associations, can reverse this natural order of things and we declare unhesitatingly that to reverse them is the first and most natural desire of San Francisco."[2]

The *Record-Union's* declaration was representative of the growing belief in mankind's inability to control events by conscious

In 1891-92 the Southern Pacific's long wharf at *Port Los Angeles*, north of Santa Monica, was built. Huntington had lobbied in Congress to make this the official port to be improved at government expense. — DONALD DUKE COLLECTION

effort. Faith in the inevitable march of history toward a "natural" end was also the philosophy of a railroad employee who told a California legislative committee in 1893: "All those who throw themselves in the way of the wheels of progress will be crushed sooner or later; they cannot stop it; you nor I nor any one else can control the question."[3] To a large degree, it was also the view of California's Frank Norris, who wrote in *The Octopus* (1901) of fictional sheep and men, slaughtered for standing in the path of the locomotive.

The famous novelist was vague concerning the "natural" end toward which events were moving. But he did insist through his novel's characters that not even the Southern Pacific, for all its control of railroad commissions and legislatures, could control events. Here he was historically accurate, for in the context of the Southern Pacific's world, all was not victory. For one thing, the Big Four were dying off. Crocker followed Hopkins to the grave in 1888. Stanford died in 1893 and Huntington in 1900, although not before an open quarrel between the two. Huntington's private correspondence reveals that at an early date in their business affairs he developed a strong dislike for Stanford. He held this in relative silence for many years, but following Stanford's election to the United States Senate in 1885 Huntington publicly charged his partner with bribing his way to the federal upper house.[4] Thereafter, until Stanford's death, internal strife plagued the company. Meanwhile, the old problem of the Central Pacific's debt to the federal government had also been coming to a climax. In the years following the Thurman Act of 1878, the managers of the Central Pacific had minimized the annual amount paid to the government by diverting most of their business to the Southern Pacific's sunset route. However, this ruse merely postponed the company's ultimate settlement with the federal treasury. In the closing years of the 19th century, Huntington could find no new evasive maneuver to fall back on, and an agreement was made for the final payment of the debt.[5]

In addition to these problems, the Southern Pacific lost a lengthy battle with the people of Los Angeles in the 1890's over the site of a harbor to be improved at federal expense. Huntington had lobbied in Congress for Santa Monica, whose port facilities

Congress and Los Angeles favored the development of San Pedro harbor, as opposed to Southern Pacific's Port Los Angeles. Terminal Island was already busy with activity in this turn of the century illustration. — DONALD DUKE COLLECTION

The busy Southern Pacific roundhouse in Los Angeles in 1891 testified that the community was becoming an important rail center of southern California. — DONALD DUKE COLLECTION

were owned by the Southern Pacific. Most Angelinos had favored San Pedro, which was not controlled by any one road. Congress finally selected San Pedro, a decision influenced by several reports of government engineers. Work on the harbor began in April 1899. Los Angeles had beaten the Southern Pacific, but the victory was only temporary. Following the sale of the company to Edward H. Harriman upon the death of Huntington, the Southern Pacific came to absorb much of the terminal facilities at San Pedro.[6] Even in defeat, the Southern Pacific managed to retain the appearance of control, giving it a reputation for invincibility.

Nevertheless, a new age was forming in which neither localities nor railroad corporations dominated economic events.[7] Localities, such as San Diego, had discovered that it no longer paid to mortgage their futures to promote railroad development, for the benefited companies operated under the harsh economic realities of national competition and could not sacrifice profits to favor any particular community. Other cities also painfully learned that the tactics of the sixties and seventies were no longer suited to the national economic conditions at the turn of the century, for not even mighty San Francisco could successfully manipulate national commerce to preserve its old favored status. As in California, so across the nation, a community-oriented society was no longer capable of achieving its desires by traditional methods, and this realization bred a dark mood. Californians read *The Octopus* and reflected on one of its character's description of the railroad as "a force born out of certain conditions." "No man can stop it or control it," uttered the novel's fictional counterpart of Huntington.[7] Californians, as did other Americans of that generation, found this attitude both dangerous and attractive. Fatalism could soothe the pain of continuing failure to control events in a society seemingly adrift, yet the readers of *The Octopus* also sensed the threat to democratic society in such a philosophy of life. Contemporary sociologist William Graham Sumner claimed that democracy, already altered by the pressures of industrialism, was merely a passing form and could not be maintained by the activities of men.[8] The first generation of the new century would respond to this challenge of despair.

NOTES

1. Stuart Daggett, *Chapters on the History of the Southern Pacific* (Berkeley, 1922), p. 315.
2. *Sacramento Record-Union,* Oct. 12, 1891, 2:2.
3. California Senate Committee on Constitutional Amendments, *Report of the Testimony and Proceedings Taken Before the Senate Committee on Constitutional Amendments, Relative to Senate Constitutional Amendment No. 8, Abrogating Provisions of Constitution as to Railroad Commission, and Placing Distance Tariff in Constitution* (Sacramento, 1893), p. 108.
4. Charles Edward Russell, "Scientific Corruption of Politics," *Hampton's Magazine,* XXIV (1910), 854.
5. Daggett, *Southern Pacific,* pp. 389-390, 391-392, 393, 395-424; Neill C. Wilson and Frank J. Taylor, *Southern Pacific, The Roaring Story of a Fighting Railroad* (New York, 1952), pp. 241-242.
6. Franklyn Hoyt, "Railroad Development in Southern California, 1868 to 1900" (Doctoral dissertation, University of Southern California, 1951), pp. 411-414; Richard W. Barsness, "Railroads and Los Angeles: The Quest for a Deep-Water Port," *Southern California Quarterly,* XLVII (1965), pp. 389-390; Charles Dwight Willard, *A History of the Chamber of Commerce of Los Angeles, California, From its Foundation, Sept., 1888, to the year 1900* (Los Angeles, 1899), pp. 17, 130-142.
7. Communities in other parts of the nation experienced the transition from the urban imperial system to a national economy earlier than San Francisco. For

example, in the 1870's, Kansas Citians rebelled against railroad pooling agreements by promoting narrow-gauge and water-freight competition that would be operated in the interests of their city. As with the later efforts of San Francisco, their attempts ended in failure. Charles N. Glaab, the historian of Kansas City's railroad era, concludes: "As railroads became national businesses, local community programs could no longer seriously affect the location of major railroad lines or the practices of railroad companies." A realization of this among dissatisfied business groups from a number of previously rival cities encouraged a new cooperation in bringing railroad corporations under governmental controls beneficial to the general public, rather than any one urban commercial empire. See Charles N. Glaab, *Kansas City and the Railroads, Community Policy in the Growth of a Regional Metropolis* (Madison, Wisconsin, 1962), pp. 173-192.

8. Frank Norris, *The Octopus* (New York, 1901 [Bantam Book Edition, 1958]), p. 386.

9. The concepts of a "community-oriented society" and "a society seemingly adrift" are borrowed from Robert Wiebe's *The Search for Order, 1877-1920* (New York, 1967). For a concise description of William Graham Sumner's ideas see: Ralph Henry Gabriel, *The Course of American Democratic Thought* (New York, 1956), pp. 237-241.

PART
SIX

An Era Ends

Southern California's greatest boom was that of the 1880's. Thousands of persons in the East were enticed to visit the West. The railroads had land to sell, so their interest in causing the East to move West was real. By the turn of the century, 1,485,000 people lived in California, and the next decade would see a 60 percent leap in the State's population. The Santa Fe Railway organized the California Excursion Assn. to turn the attention of the United States to southern California. In this scene the young frolic over dinner aboard a Santa Fe Fred Harvey operated diner en route to California. — DONALD DUKE COLLECTION

16

The Progressive Response

BY the turn of the century, the Southern Pacific's influence in California politics was apparent. Railroad Commissions and State Boards of Equalization, the latter assessing the Southern Pacific for taxation, had been controlled. Some legislators had been corrupted for single acts; others, like Hiram Johnson's father Grove, were company regulars. Governors had served the Big Four by vetoing bills that filtered through semi-corrupted legislatures. Local, state, and federal courts had been used as the last defensive shield of the company; and jurists such as Stephen Field and Joseph McKenna, both long-time personal friends of Leland Stanford, rarely disappointed the Southern Pacific. Railroad agents were to be found in local politics as well, for county assessors needed to be controlled to minimize local taxes on the corporation's many interests. Local political organizations·were also important to the company as spawning places of loyal congressmen and state legislators. And urban bosses such as Christopher Buckley, who fell from power in the early 1890's, were useful in many capacities.[1]

Despite their obvious presence in California politics, the company's directors periodically voiced a reluctance to remain in political life and issued proclamations of withdrawal. "That is the great

Alternately labeled *Herrin's Cabinet* and *The Shame of California*, the above photograph first appeared in the *San Francisco Call* on September 10, 1906. James N. Gillett appears in the center with his hand on Abraham Ruef's left shoulder. Walter Parker is standing immediately to Gillett's left. Judge Kerrigan appears second from the right.

— Wrightwood Collection

thing, to get the road out of politics," Charles Crocker asserted with some sincerity in 1887. When the Huntington-Stanford quarrel exploded a year later, more evidence of the Southern Pacific's corruption of the state surfaced, bringing with it promises by Huntington not to interfere further with the governmental process. By 1891, his subordinates ostensibly were being told to keep "the hand of the railroad" out of the California legislature. Two decades later, the Southern Pacific's William F. Herrin claimed that his company slowly dismantled its political organization following Leland Stanford's death in 1893. Certainly Stanford's involvement in politics often went beyond merely serving the needs of his company. His election to the Senate at a time when other functionaries could have filled the role showed that. It would logically follow, then, that his death could have brought about some degree of retrenchment in the Southern Pacific's political life. The weakening of the state railroad commission by McKenna's court in the decade of Stanford's death also gave credence to Herrin's claim, for the Southern Pacific had no reason to corrupt a virtually powerless body.[2]

Nevertheless, few contemporary observers could accept the claim that the railroad had withdrawn from politics. Firm evidence of corruption, unearthed by the *San Francisco Call* in September 1906 and later substantiated by one of the principal parties involved, proved indeed that Herrin and the Southern Pacific were still soiling the state's political nests. At the Republican state nominating convention that year, Herrin paid $14,000 to Abraham Ruef, political boss of San Francisco, to cast the votes of his delegation for James N. Gillett, the company's choice for governor. A damning photograph was circulated by the press, showing Gillett, Ruef, Judge Kerrigan, and Walter Parker (the company's manager of southern California politics) posing with a few others at a victory celebration following Gillett's nomination. Labeled "Herrin's cabinet," this photograph was used with effect by the new century's progressive reformers to anger the public from its lethargy.[3]

California's "progressives" felt that they could symbolically recapture control of events by kicking the Southern Pacific out of California politics.[4] They also believed that real economic control could be attained by instituting effective state-wide rate regulation. With railroad corporations no longer operating in the interests of

E. H. Harriman

By combining the Southern Pacific with other important lines, E. H. Harriman created a rail system symbolic of a new, complex economic situation which appeared beyond human control. Frank Norris fictionalized this belief in *The Octopus* (1901). Joseph McKenna, a loyal friend of the Southern Pacific on the bench, closely resembled the fictional Judge Ulsteen of Norris's novel. — Union Pacific Collection

Frank Norris

Joseph McKenna

particular communities, a tough state commission could force the railroads to act in the interests of the state at large. Other states were creating new commissions, which deliberately and systematically set intrastate rate structures to discriminate against merchants and producers of other states. In an age of consolidation of railroad facilities, of which Edward H. Harriman's combination of the Union Pacific and Southern Pacific systems was a key example, a strong state commission could be just as valuable in maintaining or expanding the commercial empires of localities as city-backed railroad schemes had been in an earlier era.[5]

By 1909, pressure for this kind of reform was so great in Sacramento that even Governor Gillett felt impelled to call for a legislative revitalization of California's Railroad Commission and all necessary measures to end long-standing railroad abuses. The progressives in the 1909 legislative session responded with the Stetson bill. Designed in part to effectively outlaw the rebate, the bill proposed to give the commission power to set absolute rates rather than simply maximum ones. But since the reformers lacked the necessary votes, the final result was the passage of the much less effective and railroad-backed Wright bill.[6] However, the progressives fought on, for conditions were ripe for reform. In the past, attempts in California to develop strong state control over railroad rates had been weakened by intrastate local jealousies. But by the end of the new century's first decade, few California communities were without railroad facilities. And discrimination among communities, long a divisive factor in California's railroad politics, was also ebbing. The outrageous discrimination described in *The Octopus*, of freight sent past its destination to San Francisco and back before it finally could be delivered, ended with the proliferation of terminal points brought about by transcontinental competition.[7] As communities increasingly received equal treatment from railroad corporations, Californians desiring a strong Railroad Commission could work together with greater harmony.

Succeeding in electing Hiram Johnson governor in 1910, the reformers also mustered an overwhelming majority in the regular legislative session of 1911, passing a powerful Railroad Commission Act and three constitutional amendments concerning the Railroad Commission. After ratification of the amendments by the

Hiram Johnson achieved the Governor's chair in 1910 by campaigning on a platform which was hostile to the Southern Pacific. — WRIGHTWOOD COLLECTION

voters, Governor Johnson called the legislature into special session late in 1911 to enact a strong Public Utilities Act. Several alterations were made in California's scheme of rate regulation by these reforms of 1911. For example, one amendment increased the commission from three to five members to be appointed by the governor from the state at large. Under the new plan commissioners would serve six-year terms, staggered to give the commission a constant backlog of experience. Another of the amendments expanded the regulating chores of the commission to encompass most public utilities. The third amendment altered the system of regulation created in 1879 in a variety of ways. For example, the long-and-short-haul clause was made inoperative at the discretion of the commission, and provisions declared unconstitutional by the federal courts were struck from the state constitution. Finally, a section was added to the document to prevent a repetition of the Fresno Rate Case: henceforth, a California railroad could not raise rates previously lowered even in "self-defense," unless given permission by the Railroad Commission.[8]

The legislation passed in 1911 brought additional changes. For example, the commission was given the power to set absolute rates, rather than merely maximum ones. In the Fresno Rate Case, Chief Justice Beatty of the California Supreme Court had said

John Eshleman   **Leroy Wright**

Eshleman became one of the first members of the revitalized
Railroad Commission. Wright was identified with politics fa-
vorable to the railroad corporations. — WRIGHTWOOD COLLEC-
TION

that the commission could set only maximum rates, but this had
been strictly obiter dictum. Moreover, the Supreme Court of the
United States had never directly decided this issue.[9] Nevertheless,
in 1911, California's progressives were definitely willing to take
chances with the courts. Governor Johnson had told his followers:

> I beg of you not to permit the bogie man of the railroad com-
> panies, "Unconstitutionality," to deter you from enacting the
> legislation suggested. . . . Let us do our full duty, now that at
> last we have a Railroad Commission that will do its full duty,
> and let us give this Commission all the power and aid and re-
> sources it requires; and if, thereafter, legitimate work done
> within the law and the Constitution shall be nullified, let the
> consequences rest with the nullifying power.[10]

This attitude also held true for restricting judicial review of commission-set rates, which the courts had promoted in recent years.
The Public Utilities Act of 1911 affirmed that the commission's

decision would be final on questions of fact and those regarding reasonableness of rates. A provision included in one of the constitutional amendments of 1911 served as a foundation of this legislation. After the proper state procedures for due process have been exhausted, the amendment reads, commission-set rates will "not be subject to review by any court except upon the question whether such decision of the commission will result in confiscation of property."[11]

While the Southern Pacific was not without protest against these measures, contemporaries were surprised by the relative silence of the railroad politicos faced with new stringent regulation. Some thought that the company realized that its opponents had the votes to enact their measures and could not be swayed by arguments.[12] Another factor, however, must also be considered. "The new law won't hurt the railroads," said pro-railroad state Senator Leroy Wright, casting his ballot for the Railroad Commission Act of 1911. He also hinted to reporters that all railroad rates might soon be regulated by the federal government, thus making the passage of a new scheme of state regulation a bogus victory.[13] In short, the railroad was willing to tolerate a temporary victory by the California progressives, for it believed that the federal government would soon make intrastate railroad rate regulation a national affair. Apparently others held this same belief. Commenting on a statement made by Interstate Commerce Commissioner Franklin K. Lane in 1911 that state regulation was an anachronism, California Railroad Commissioner John M. Eshleman politely and prophetically conceded that an era of local influence in railroad affairs was inevitably passing in favor of a more efficient order:

> I am glad to say that before I had listened to the eloquent words of Commissioner Lane, I had already reached the conclusion, which is the inevitable conclusion which anybody reaches who studies this question, that it is best for all concerned that one central body regulate the entire length and breadth of the railroad where it traverses more than one State. . . . We will come ultimately to a federal regulation of railroads. There is no question of it.[14]

Fearing *nationalization* of their industry, the railroads were willing to meet the public "halfway," and they apparently thought that the Interstate Commerce Commission would be the best instrument of compromise.[15] In 1911, the first step toward nationalizing rate *regulation* was taken. Two months after the passage of the Railroad Commission Act, a federal circuit court handed down a decision affirming federal authority over intrastate rates. This case was then taken to the Supreme Court in the *Minnesota Rate Cases* (1913), where an approximation of the lower court's interpretation of the I.C.C.'s powers over intrastate rates was given in an obiter dictum of Justice Hughes. Moreover, in the *Shreveport Rate Cases* (1914), the court directly upheld the federal commission's power to regulate intrastate rail rates.[16] Railroad men were satisfied with these developments. On the other hand, many state railroad commissioners concluded that the court's decision of 1914 had made their job of regulating intrastate rates "an impossible one," thus killing the last great attempt to maintain local control over railroad affairs. Six years later in the Transportation Act of 1920, Congress confirmed the I.C.C.'s powers over the state railroad commissions. After this, the California Railroad Commission (Public Utilities Commission) shifted most of its attention from railroads to other public utilities.[17] The state had reached the end of an era, characterized by corporate and public disorganization in transportation affairs, and during which community conflicts had played a distinguishing role.

NOTES

1. Dumas Malone, ed., *Dictionary of American Biography* (New York, 1933), VI, 88; Carl B. Swisher, *Stephen J. Field, Craftsman of the Law* (Hamden, Conn., 1930), pp. 240-267; Democratic Party of California, State Central Committee, *The Railroad is an Issue in Politics* (San Francisco, 1898), pp. 5-9; Alexander Callow, Jr., "San Francisco's Blind Boss," *Pacific Historical Review*, XXV (1956), 277.

2. *Testimony Taken by the United States Pacific Railway Commission, Appointed Under the Act of Congress Approved March 3, 1887, Entitled 'An Act Authorizing an Investigation of the Books, Accounts, and Methods of Railroads Which Have Received Aid From the United States, and Other Purposes'* (Washington, 1887), VII, 3684; "The Railroad Out of Politics," *The Wave*, VI (1891), 10; Robert Glass Cleland, *A History of California: The American Period* (New York, 1922), p. 438. A recent biography of Stanford makes a strong case that Stanford's nomination to the U.S. Senate in 1885 was unsought by him and was only accepted to unite the Republican Party: see Norman E. Tutorow, *Leland Stanford: Man of Many Careers* (Menlo Park, 1971), pp. 244-250.

3. Charles Edward Russell, "The Railroad Machine As It Works Now," *Hampton's Magazine*, XXV (1910), 368, 370; George Mowry, *The California Progressives* (Berkeley, 1951), pp. 29-30; Walton Bean, *Boss Ruef's San Francisco, The Story of the Union Labor Party, Big Business, and the Graft Prosecution* (Berkeley, 1952), pp. 145-152.
4. Spencer C. Olin, Jr., *California's Prodigal Sons, Hiram Johnson and the Progressives, 1911-1917* (Berkeley, 1968), p. 26.
5. George Kennan, *E. H. Harriman, A Biography* (New York, 1922), I, 238-240, 283; William Z. Ripley, *Railroads: Rates and Regulation* (New York, 1912), pp. 487-488, 629; James R. Norvell, "The Railroad Commission of Texas: Its Origin and History," *Southwestern Historical Quarterly*, LXVIII (1965), 473-474.
6. Franklin Hichborn, *Story of the Session of the California Legislature of 1909* (San Francisco, 1909), pp. 137-143; *Mowry, California Progressives*, p. 81; Gerald Nash, *State Government and Economic Development, A History of Administrative Policies in California, 1849-1933* (Berkeley, 1964), 253-254.
7. In the early years of the Central Pacific, only San Francisco, San Jose, and Sacramento were designated "terminal points," receiving rates lower than other communities in the State. Then in the 1870's, Stockton was made a terminal point, and with the growth of railroad facilities and transcontinental competition, many more towns received terminal point benefits. By 1910, 97 California communities were terminal points. See: Stuart Daggett, *Chapters on the History of the Southern Pacific* (Berkeley, 1922), pp. 281-282.
8. Eugene Hallett, comp., *Public Utilities Act of California* (San Francisco, 1912), pp. 155-159, 161-162.
9. *Report of the Railroad Commission of California, From January 1, 1911 to June 30, 1912* (Sacramento, 1912), pp. 471-498; Franklin Hichborn, *Story of the Session of the California Legislature of 1911* (San Francisco, 1911), p. 146; Hichborn, *Story of California Legislature of 1909*, p. 136; H. S. Smalley, "Railway Rate Control in its Legal Aspects," *American Economic Association Publication*, VII (1906), 347.
10. *The Journal of the Assembly, Thirty-Ninth Session* (Sacramento, 1911), p. 49.
11. *The Statutes of California and Amendments to the Constitution Passed at the Extra Session of the Session of the Thirty-Ninth Legislature* (Sacramento, 1912), pp. 55-56; Hallett, comp., *Public Utilities Act*, p. 155. These enactments clearly were not harmonious with the Supreme Court decision of *Smyth v. Ames* (1898), 169 U.S. 466. That case had firmly enunciated that the courts would protect railroad companies not only from state confiscation of their property without just compensation but also from state-set rates which would not produce a "reasonable" profit. And it is the judiciary's job, said the court, to decide what is a reasonable profit. This is where the court stood in regard to rates set by state railroad commissions. But in regard to the Interstate Commerce Commission, a new body of constitutional law was appearing. In January, 1910, the Supreme Court ruled that judicial investigations into rates set by the I.C.C. could only be justified on the grounds that such rates were confiscatory. Reasonable profit was to be a matter decided solely by the commission. (See: *Interstate Commerce Commission v. Illinois Central Railroad Co.*, 215 U.S. 452). The California progressives were willing to gamble that if and when the reform of 1911 came to court the judges would apply similar reasoning to a case involving state regulation. (See: "The Railroad Commission Amendments," *Transactions of the Commonwealth Club of California*, VI (1911), 255). In effect, the reformers were saying that a question of reasonableness would be *conclusive* with the Railroad Commission, leaving as *prima facie* evidence only questions involving con-

230

fiscation. The principle of narrow judicial review of state-set rates came before the Supreme Court in the *Minnesota Rate Cases* (1913), 230 U.S. 352, and the court handed down a decision quite harmonious with the new California reform.

12. "The Railroad Commission Amendments," *Commonwealth Club*, pp. 251, 271; Franklin Hichborn, *Story of the Session of the California Legislature of 1911*, pp. 147-149; *San Francisco Bulletin*, Jan. 2, 1911, 8:2.
13. *Los Angeles Times*, Feb. 9, 1911, 2:4.
14. "The Railroad Commission Amendments," *Commonwealth Club*, pp. 263-264.
15. E. P. Ripley, "The Railroads and the People," *Atlantic Monthly*, CVII (1911), 22. The railroads wanted stability that could only come with national regulation. Gabriel Kolko has well documented the growing movement among railroad men to make regulation national; see his *Railroads and Regulation, 1877-1916* (Princeton, 1965), pp. 147-148, 151, 219-220, 223. Nevertheless, Kolko exaggerates the community of interest between the railroad companies and the Interstate Commerce Commission. Albro Martin's *Enterprise Denied, Origins of the Decline of American Railroads, 1897-1917* (New York, 1971) [pp. 38-50, 352] corrects Kolko but also exaggerates in portraying the I.C.C. as the arch-enemy of the railroads. The strengthening of the I.C.C. was in fact a compromise that fully satisfied neither the extremists in control of the state regulatory commissions nor the railroad companies.
16. *Minnesota Rate Cases*, 184 Fed. Rep. 765. See California's reaction to this in *California Outlook*, X (1911), 3-4, and *San Francisco Call*, April 2, 1912, 4:1; *Minnesota Rate Cases* 230 U.S. 352; *Houston & Texas Railway Co. v. United States*, 234 U.S. 342; Walter D. Hines, "The Conflict Between State and Federal Regulation of Railroads," *Annals of the American Academy of Political and Social Science*, LXIII (1916), 191-196; James R. Norvell, "The Railroad Commission of Texas," pp. 473-474.
17. *Railway Age Gazette*, LVI (1914), 1260; Edward S. Corwin, "Making Railroad Regulation National," *New Republic*, II (1915), 95-96; Kolko, *Railroads and Regulation*, pp. 229-230; Nash, *State Government and Economic Development*, pp. 251, 264.

During 1905 the Colorado River burst its bounds with the first of a long series of floods that almost washed the Imperial Valley into the Salton Sink which was becoming an inland sea. Southern Pacific forces worked two years returning the river to its proper channel. In this scene, a Southern Pacific passenger train rolls across a temporary bridge crossing the Salton Sea inlet near Salton.—DONALD DUKE COLLECTION

17

Epilogue

RAILROADS did not cease to influence California history after the state's progressive reformers finished their work. The Southern Pacific continued its old lobby in Sacramento, but its political influence was reduced to special interest lobbying after the Interstate Commerce Commission entered the field of *intrastate* rate making. The company no longer thought it worthwhile to seek control of California's government. An era of the railroad's political dominance of California had ended.

Even in a more important sense, the 20th century's first decade marked the end of an era, as local rivalries in railroad affairs ebbed considerably, a result of the growing maturity of the state's railroad system. Few communities were without rail facilities by the time Hiram Johnson took office. Likewise, rate discrimination between communities lessened as scores of California towns became terminal points. If the railroad ambitions of California's communities had not been completely realized by that time, they had been tempered by partial achievement and a growing public awareness of the complexities of railroad economics.

The advent of the automobile also contributed to the sharp decline in local rivalries in railroad matters, for the extent of a community's railroad facilities increasingly was no longer the sole test of its commercial potential. As early as 1910 over 36,000 motor vehicles travelled California's primitive roads; in fact, Hiram Johnson used one of them in his campaign for governor that year, in order to dramatize his independence from the Southern Pacific. As the state's automobile and truck population continued to grow at a phenomenal rate, local rivalries had a new focus as communities competed for California's highway development funds.[1]

A new transportation era, which would be characterized by national problems rather than local ambitions, had begun. Community conflicts in transportation matters certainly lived on, but they did not typify the new era as they had the old. The march of industrialization, of which modern transportation development is a part, led away from a focus on local desires to one more concerned with national and international needs. World war and mobilization of transportation resources for defense purposes, national and international economic depression and unionization of workers, global competition among rival forms of transportation are events that dominate the story of the era that followed.

Living in this new transportation age, we are at an advantage in seeing what was most distinctive about California's bygone railroad era. Participants of that time, viewing their current events with the myopia that accompanies contemporary evaluation, saw the greed and power of men like Huntington and Stanford as the trademark of their period. Yet even Frank Norris, who did more to popularize this interpretation than any other, admitted its inadequacy for explaining the age. "If you want to fasten blame . . . on any one person, you will make a mistake," spoke Norris's fictional counterpart of Huntington. "Blame conditions, not men."[2]

California's railroad era was shaped by conditions that were both shared with the rest of the nation and unique to the far west. The era had started at a time of national industrial "take-off," during which men and communities lived with a fear that they would be left behind. Concurrently, the period marked the development of the far west, which grew in population and wealth at a greater pace than the rest of the country. Local rivalries, which would characterize California's railroad era, were greatly accentuated by the dovetailing of these two conditions.

234

At the commencement of California's railroad era, local jealousies contributed to the lack of action on a transcontinental railroad. As soon as the project was subsidized by Congress, they largely obstructed its progress. After its completion, local ambitions and conflicts blocked the selection of the terminus favored by the Central Pacific. Later, local rivalries spurred the construction of the Southern Pacific and other roads with city and county subsidies. Concurrently, they kept the state legislature from enacting effective rate regulation and helped persuade the state constitutional convention that the matter of regulation could effectively be handled only by a commission, which would be largely free from such bickering. However, the writing of this reform into the state constitution made change thereafter more difficult, a situation which was fully exploited by the Big Four. When the coming of transcontinental railroad competition radically changed old relationships between companies and their past urban backers, some communities, such as San Diego, became clouded with disillusionment. Others, like San Francisco, rebelled and unsuccessfully tried to halt the new order, and in failing nurtured a mood of fatalism concerning "the Octopus." In turn, this belief challenged democracy's advocates to enact long-awaited reforms at the dawn of a new century. These reforms would quickly be undermined, not by the centrifugal desires of local rivalries which had characterized the American industrial revolution during its early years, but rather by new centralized solutions which seemed to lead away from a growing disorder.

NOTES

1. Paul E. Vandor, *History of Fresno County, California* (Los Angeles, 1919), p. 310; *Fact Book, Department of Motor Vehicles, State of California* (Sacramento, 1965), p. 7.
2. Frank Norris, *The Octopus* (New York, 1901 [Bantum Book Edition, 1958]), p. 386.

Bibliography

NEWSPAPERS AND PERIODICALS

California Outlook, 1911. Los Angeles.
Daily Alta California, 1851-1878. San Francisco.
Los Angeles Times, 1911. Los Angeles.
Los Angeles Weekly Express, 1876-1878. Los Angeles.
Railway Age Gazette, 1914. New York.
Sacramento Record-Union, 1876-1891. Sacramento.
San Diego News, 1878. San Diego.
San Diego Union, 1876. San Diego.
San Francisco Bulletin, 1868-1911. San Francisco.
San Francisco Call, 1912. San Francisco.
San Francisco Chronicle, 1874-1879. San Francisco.
San Francisco Examiner, 1893-1898. San Francisco.
San Luis Obispo Tribune, 1876. San Luis Obispo.

COLLECTED DOCUMENTS, LETTERS, NOTES, AND CLIPPINGS

Bancroft Scraps, Vols. XXXII, LXVI, LXXX. Located at Bancroft Library, University of California, Berkeley.

Daggett, Stuart. California Railroad Notes, ca. 1850-1932. 3 cartons (141 packets). Bancroft Library, University of California, Berkeley.

Hopkins, Mark, et al. *Letters from Mark Hopkins, Leland Stanford, Charles Crocker, Charles F. Crocker, and David D. Colton, to Collis P. Huntington, From Aug. 27, 1869 to Dec. 30, 1879.* New York, 1891.

Hopkins, Timothy. Random Notes on Central Pacific History. Hopkins Transportation Library, Stanford University, California.

Huntington, Collis P. *Letters from Collis P. Huntington to Mark Hopkins, Leland Stanford, Charles Crocker, E. B. Crocker, Charles F. Crocker, and David D. Colton.* 3 vols. New York, 1892-1894.

Huntington MSS, 1867-1872. Microfilm, Huntington Library, San Marino, California.

Leland Stanford Correspondence, 1867-1869. Stanford University Library, Stanford, California.

PAMPHLETS, SPEECHES, REPORTS, AND MEMORIALS

Browne, John Ross. *The Policy of Extending Local Aid to Railroads, With Special Reference to the Proposed Line Through the San Joaquin Valley to the Colorado River.* San Francisco, 1870.

Central Pacific Railroad Co. (John Scott). *Information Concerning the Terminus of the Railroad System of the Pacific Coast.* Oakland, 1871.

Commonwealth Club of California. "The Railroad Commission Amendments." *Transactions of the Commonwealth Club of California,* VI (1911), 237-273.

————. "The Railroad Commission of California." *Transactions of the Commonwealth Club of California,* III (1908), 321-392.

Delta Printing Establishment. *The Struggle of the Mussel Slough Settlers for their Homes! An Appeal to the People.* Visalia, 1880.

Democratic Party of California, State Central Committee. *The Railroad is an Issue in Politics. San Francisco,* 1898.

Doyle, John T. *Railroad Rates and Transportation Overland. In a Letter (March 25, 1881) to a Member of Congress.* San Francisco, 1893.

George, Henry. *The Subsidy Question and the Democratic Party.* n.p., 1871.

The Great Dutch Flat Swindle! The City of San Francisco Demands Justice! The Matter in Controversy, and the Present State of the Question. An Address to the Board of Supervisors, Officers and People of San Francisco. San Francisco, 1864.

Green, Thomas Jefferson. *Letter of Hon. Robert J. Walker, Upon the Subject of Pacific Railroad, Sept. 19, 1853.* New York, 1853.

Haight, Henry H. *Address Delivered at Sacramento, 1869, Upon the Completion of the Pacific Railroad.* San Francisco, 1869.

Hunt, Rockwell, *Golden Jubilee of the Pacific Railroad.* n.p., n.d.

Judah, Theodore. *A Practical Plan for Building the Pacific Railroad.* Washington D.C., 1857.

————. *Report of Theodore D. Judah, Accredited Agent [of the] Pacific Railroad Convention, Upon his Operations in the Atlantic States.* San Francisco, 1860.

Memorial [of the Citizens of San Francisco to the California State Legislature] Upon the Subject of Constructing a Railroad from the Pacific to the Valley of the Mississippi. Sacramento, 1853.

The Pacific Railroad, A Defense Against Its Enemies, With Report of the Supervisors of Placer County, and Report of Mr. Montanya. San Francisco, 1864.

San Francisco Chamber of Commerce. *Annual Report of the Chamber of Commerce of San Francisco, 1881-1892.* San Francisco.

San Francisco Daily Morning Call Co. *Fettered Commerce, How the Pacific Mail and the Railroads Have Bled San Francisco.* San Francisco, 1892.

San Francisco and Marysville Railroad Co. *Reports of the Board of Directors and Chief Engineer.* Marysville, 1860.

Stevens, Isaac I. *Letter of Isaac I. Stevens, Delegate from Washington Territory, to the Railroad Convention of Washington and Oregon, Called to Meet at Vancouver, W. T., May 20, 1860.* Washington City, 1860.

Vrooman, Henry. "Address on Railroads, Prepared for Delivery Before the California State Senate, Extra Session of 1884." Typed copy at Timothy Hopkins Library, Stanford University.

Winton, Hon. N. W. *Pacific Railroad Speech in the Nevada Senate, Feb. 27, 1865.* Carson City, Nev., 1865.

STATISTICAL SOURCES

California State Agricultural Society. *Transactions of the California State Agricultural Society, 1874-1876.* Sacramento.

Central Pacific Railroad Co. *Local Freight Tariff, June 22, 1873.* Hopkins Transportation Library, Stanford University, California.

Department of Motor Vehicles, State of California. *Fact Book, Department of Motor Vehicles, State of California.* Sacramento, 1965.

Southern Pacific Railroad Co. *Local Freight Tariff, To Take Effect January 1, 1875.* California State Archives, Sacramento, California.

GOVERNMENT DOCUMENTS
A. UNITED STATES DOCUMENTS

Budd v. New York, 143 U.S. 517 (1892).

Chicago and Grand Trunk Railroad v. Wellman, 143 U.S. 339 (1892).

Chicago, Milwaukee, and St. Paul Railway Co. v. Minnesota, 134 U.S. 418 (1890).

Congressional Globe, 33rd to 39th Congresses. Washington, 1853-1867.

Houston & Texas Railway Co. v. United States, 234 U.S. 342 (1914).

Interstate Commerce Commission v. Illinois Central Railroad Co., 215 U.S. 452 (1910).

Minnesota Rate Cases, 184 Fed. Rep. 765 (1911); 230 U.S. 352 (1913).

Reagan v. Farmers' Loan and Trust Company, 154 U.S. 362 (1894).

Smyth v. Ames, 169 U.S. 466 (1898).

Southern Pacific Co. v. Board of Railroad Commissioners of California et al., 78 Fed. Rep. 236 (1896).

Stone v. Farmers' Loan and Trust Company, 116 U.S. 307 (1886).

Trustees of Dartmouth College v. Woodward, 4 Wheaton 518 (1819).

United States Pacific Railway Commission. *Testimony Taken by the United States Pacific Railway Commission, Appointed Under the Act of Congress Approved March 3, 1887, Entitled 'An Act Authorizing an Investigation of the Books, Accounts, and Methods of Railroads Which Have Received Aid from the United States, and For Other Purposes.'* 6 vols. Washington, 1887.

B. City, County, and State Documents

California Assembly Committee on Corporations. *Report of the Committee on Corporations of the Assembly of the State of California Upon Railroad Freights and Fares.* Sacramento, 1871.

————. *Report of the Committee on Corporations of the Assembly of California, Twenty-Fifth Session, 1883.* Sacramento, 1883.

California Assembly Committee on Federal Relations. *Report of the Committee on Federal Relations on the Pacific Railroad, Submitted March 24, 1856.* Sacramento, 1856.

California Railroad [Transportation] Commission. *Annual Reports, 1877-1912.* Sacramento.

California Senate Committee on Commerce and Navigation. *Report of the Committee on Commerce and Navigation.* Sacramento, 1858.

California Senate Committee on Constitutional Amendments. *Report of the Testimony and Proceedings Taken Before the Senate Committee on Constitutional Amendments, Relative to Senate Constitutional Amendment No. 8, Abrogating Provisions of Constitution as to Railroad Commission, and Placing Distance Tariff in Constitution.* Sacramento, 1893.

California Senate Committee on Corporations. "Majority Report of the Committee on Corporations in Relation to Fares and Freights on Railroads." *Appendix to Journals of Senate and Assembly, of the Seventeenth Session of the Legislature of the State of California.* Vol. II. Sacramento, 1868.

————. "Majority Report of the Committee on Corporations Relative to Senate Bill No. 62." *Appendix to Journals of Senate and Assembly of the Eighteenth Session of the Legislature of the State of California.* Vol. II. Sacramento, 1870.

————. *Report of the Testimony and Proceedings Had Before the Senate Committee on Corporations, Having Under Consideration the Subject of Fares and Freights.* Sacramento, 1874.

————. *Railroad Fares and Freights, Report of the Senate Committee on Corporations, On Senate Bills Nos. 332, 319, and 334, and Assembly Bill No. 182.* Sacramento, 1876.

California Senate Committee on Federal Relations. *Report of the*

Committee on Federal Relations. Sacramento, 1853.

Ellen M. Colton v. Leland Stanford et al., Testimony (Arguments in the Superior Court of the State of California, in and for the County of Sonoma, 1883-1884). Vols. IV, XV. n.p., n.d.

Committee on Railroads of the First Nevada Legislature. *Evidence Concerning Projected Railways Across the Sierra Nevada Mountains*. Carson City, 1865.

Debates and Proceedings of the Constitutional Convention of the State of California, Convened at the City of Sacramento, Saturday, September 28, 1878. 3 vols. Sacramento, 1881.

In the District Court of the Fourth Judicial District, of the State of California, in and for the city and county of San Francisco. John R. Robinson, Plaintiff, vs. the Central Pacific Railroad Company of California et al., Defendants. Complaint. [By] *Alfred A. Cohen, Delos Lake, Attorneys for Plaintiff*. San Francisco, 1876.

E. B. Edson et al., Board of Railroad Commissioners of California, Appellants v. Southern Pacific Railroad Company, Respondents, 144 California Reports 182; or 77 Pacific Reporter 894.

Haight, Henry H. *Message of Governor H. H. Haight, Returning Without Approval Senate Bills Nos. 243 and 244, Relative to Empower Certain Counties to Aid in the Construction of Railroads*. Sacramento, 1870.

Hallett, Eugene, comp. *Public Utilities Act of California*. San Francisco, 1912.

The Journal of the Assembly of the State of California, 6th to 39th sessions. Sacramento, 1855-1911.

The Journal of the Senate of the State of California, 16th to 25th sessions. Sacramento, 1866-1884.

Pardee, George C. "Second Biennial Message of Governor George C. Pardee." *Appendix to Journals of Senate and Assembly, California, Thirty-Seventh Session — 1907*, I, 48-49. Sacramento, 1907.

The People ex rel. the Attorney General v. J. Neely Johnson et al., 6 Calif. Reports 499 (1856).

Statutes of California, 1873-1912. Sacramento.

Surveyor General of California. *Annual Report of the Surveyor General*, 1852-1856. Sacramento.

COUNTY AND STATE HISTORIES

Bancroft, Hubert Howe. *History of California*. Vols. IV-VII. San Francisco, 1886-1890.

Cleland, Robert Glass. *A History of California: The American Period*. New York, 1922.

Delay, Peter J. *History of Yuba and Sutter Counties, California*. Los Angeles, 1924.

Elliot, Wallace W. *History of San Bernardino and San Diego Counties, California, 1883*. Riverside, Calif.; 1965: reprint.

Guinn, James. *Historical and Biographical Record of Southern California from its Earliest Settlement to the Opening Year of the Twentieth Century*. Chicago, 1902.

————. *A History of California and an Extended History of Its Southern Coast Counties*. Vol. I. Los Angeles, 1907.

Hittell, Theodore H. *History of California*. Vol. IV. San Francisco, 1897.

Ingersoll, Luther A. *Ingersoll's Century Annals of San Bernardino County, 1769 to 1904*. Los Angeles, 1904.

The Lewis Publishing Company. *An Illustrated History of Los Angeles County, California*. Chicago, 1889.

————. *An Illustrated History of San Joaquin County, California*. Chicago, 1890.

Mansfield, George C. *History of Butte County, California*. Los Angeles, 1918.

Menefee, Eugene L. and Fred A. Dodge. *History of Tulare and Kings Counties, Calif.* Los Angeles, 1913.

Morgan, Wallace M. *History of Kern County, California*. Los Angeles, 1914.

Sawyer, Eugene T. *History of Santa Clara County, California*. Los Angeles, 1922.

Small, Kathleen E. and J. Larry Smith. *History of Tulare County and Kings County, Calif.* Chicago, 1926.

Thompson, Thomas H. and Albert A. West. *History of Nevada, 1881*. Berkeley, 1958: reprint.

————. *Reproduction of Thompson and West's History of Santa Barbara and Ventura Counties, California*. Berkeley, 1961.

Tinkham, George. *History of San Joaquin County, California*. Los

Angeles, 1923.

Vandor, Paul E. *History of Fresno County, California. With Biographical Sketches.* Los Angeles, 1919.

Willis, William L. *History of Sacramento County, California.* Los Angeles, 1913.

MONOGRAPHS AND SPECIAL STUDIES
A. BOOKS AND DISSERTATIONS

Bancroft, Hubert Howe. *History of the Life of Leland Stanford, A Character Study.* Oakland, 1952.

Bean, Walton. *Boss Ruef's San Francisco, The Story of the Union Labor Party, Big Business, and the Graft Prosecution.* Berkeley, 1952.

Bradley, Glenn. *The Story of the Santa Fe.* Boston, 1920.

Clark, George. *Leland Stanford (1824-1893): War Governor of California. Railroad Builder and Founder of Stanford University.* Stanford, 1931.

Cole, Cornelius. *Memoirs of Cornelius Cole, Ex-Senator of the United States From California.* New York, 1908.

Daggett, Stuart. *Chapters on the History of the Southern Pacific.* Berkeley, 1922.

Dobie, Edith. *The Political Career of Stephen Mallory White. A Study of Party Activities Under the Convention System.* Stanford, 1927.

Duke, Donald and Stan Kistler. *Santa Fe, Steel Rails Through California.* San Marino, Calif., 1963.

Dumke, Glenn S. *The Boom of the Eighties in Southern California.* San Marino, Calif., 1944.

Ellison, Joseph. *California and the Nation, 1850-1869: A Study of the Relations of a Frontier Community With the Federal Government.* Berkeley, 1927.

Fahey, Frank M. "The Legislative Background of the California Constitutional Convention of 1878-1879." Unpublished Master's thesis, Stanford University, 1947.

Fankhauser, William C. *A Financial History of California, Public Revenues, Debts and Expenditures.* Berkeley, 1913.

Glaab, Charles N. *Kansas City and the Railroads, Community Policy in the Growth of a Regional Metropolis.* Madison, Wisconsin, 1962.

Greever, William S. *Arid Domain, The Santa Fe and Its Western Land Grant.* Stanford, 1954.

Griswold, Wesley S. *A Work of Giants: Building the First Transcontinental Railroad.* New York, 1962.

Grodinsky, Julius. *Transcontinental Railway Strategy, 1869-1893: A Study of Businessmen.* Philadelphia, 1962.

Hafen, Leroy. *The Overland Mail, 1849-1869.* Cleveland, 1926.

Hichborn, Franklin. *Story of the Session of the California Legislature of 1909.* San Francisco, 1909.

————. *Story of the Session of the California Legislature of 1911.* San Francisco, 1911.

————. *Story of the Session of the California Legislature of 1913.* San Francisco, 1913.

Hinckley, Helen. *Rails from the West, A Biography of Theodore D. Judah.* San Marino, California, 1969.

Hoyt, Franklyn. "Railroad Development in Southern California, 1868 to 1900." Unpublished doctoral dissertation, University of Southern California, 1951.

Jackson. W. Turrentine. *Wagon Roads West, A Study of Federal Road Surveys and Construction in the Trans-Mississippi West, 1846-1869.* Berkeley, 1952.

Josephson, Matthew. *The Robber Barons, The Great American Capitalists, 1861-1901.* New York, 1934.

Kennan, George. *E. H. Harriman, A Biography.* 2 vols. New York, 1922.

Kirkland, Edward C. *Men, Cities and Transportation, A Study in New England History, 1820-1900.* 2 vols. Cambridge, Mass., 1948.

Kolko, Gabriel. *Railroads and Regulation, 1877-1916.* Princeton, 1965.

Lavender, David. *The Great Persuader.* New York, 1970.

Lesley, Lewis B. "The Struggle of San Diego for a Southern Transcontinental Railroad Connection, 1854-1891." Unpublished doctoral dissertation, University of California, Berkeley, 1933.

Lewis, Oscar. *The Big Four*. New York, 1938.

Low, Frederick F. *Reflections of a California Governor*. Sacramento, 1959.

McAfee, Ward. "Local Interests and Railroad Regulation in Nineteenth Century California." Unpublished doctoral dissertation, Stanford University, 1966.

McCague, James. *Moguls and Iron Men, The Story of the First Transcontinental Railroad*. New York, 1964.

Marshall, James. *Santa Fe, The Railroad that Built an Empire*. New York, 1945.

Martin, Albro. *Enterprise Denied, Origins of the Decline of American Railroads, 1897-1917*. New York, 1971.

Melendy, H. Brett and Benjamin F. Gilbert. *The Governors of California, Peter H. Burnett to Edmund G. Brown*, Georgetown, Calif., 1965.

Miller, George H. "The Granger Laws, A Study of the Origins of State Railway Control in the Upper Mississippi Valley." Unpublished doctoral dissertation, University of Michigan, 1951.

Miner, H. Craig. *The St. Louis-San Francisco Transcontinental Railroad, The Thirty-Fifth Parallel Project, 1853-1890*. Lawrence, 1972.

Mowry, George E. *The California Progressives*. Berkeley, 1951.

Mudgett, Margaret H. "The Political Career of Leland Stanford." Unpublished Master's thesis, University of Southern California, 1933.

Nash, Gerald. "The Role of State Government in the Economy of California, 1849-1911." Unpublished doctoral dissertation, University of California, Berkeley, 1957.

————. *State Government and Economic Development, A History of Administrative Policies of California, 1849-1933*. Berkeley, 1964.

Olin, Spencer C., Jr. *California's Prodigal Sons, Hiram Johnson and the Progressives, 1911-1917*. Berkeley, 1968.

Quiett, Glen Chesney. *They Built the West, An Epic of Rails and Cities*. New York, 1934.

Riegel, Robert E. *The Story of Western Railroads, From 1852 Through the Reign of the Giants*. New York, 1926.

Ripley, William Z. *Railroads: Rates and Regulation*. New York,

1912.

Swisher, Carl B. *Motivation and Political Technique in the California Constitutional Convention, 1878-1879.* Claremont, Calif.; 1930.

————. *Stephen J. Field, Craftsman of the Law.* Hamden, Conn.; 1930.

Tutorow, Norman. *Leland Stanford: Man of Many Careers.* Menlo Park, 1971.

Wade, Richard C. *The Urban Frontier, The Rise of Western Cities,* 1790-1830. Cambridge, Mass.; 1959.

Waters, Lawrence Leslie. *Steel Trails to Santa Fe.* Lawrence, Kan.; 1950.

Wheeler Publishing Co. *The Valley Road, A History of the Traffic Association of California, The League of Progress, The North American Navigation Company. The Merchants Shipping Association and San Joaquin Valley Railway.* San Francisco, 1896.

Wiebe, Robert H. *The Search for Order, 1877-1920.* New York, 1967.

Willard, Charles Dwight. *A History of the Chamber of Commerce of Los Angeles, California, From Its Foundation, Sept., 1888, to the year 1900.* Los Angeles, 1899.

Wilson, Neill C. and Frank J. Taylor. *Southern Pacific, The Roaring Story of a Fighting Railroad.* New York, 1952.

Winther, Oscar O. *Express and Stagecoach Days in California.* Stanford, 1936.

B. Articles

Barsness, Richard W. "Railroads and Los Angeles: The Quest for a Deep-Water Port." *Southern California Quarterly,* XLVII (1965), 379-394.

Callow, Alexander, Jr. "San Francisco's Blind Boss." *Pacific Historical Review,* XXV (1956), 261-279.

Connolly, C. P. "Big Business and the Bench." *Everybody's Magazine,* XXVI (1912), 291-306.

Corwin, Edward S. "Making Railroad Regulation National." *New Republic,* II (1915), 94-96.

"The Courts, the Plutocracy and the People." *Arena,* XXXVI (1906), 84-87.

Ellison, William H., ed. "Memoirs of Hon. William M. Gwin." *California Historical Society Quarterly,* XIX (1940), 1-26, 157-184, 256-277, 344-367.

Goodrich, Carter. "The Revulsion Against Internal Improvements." *Journal of Economic History,* X (1950), 145-169.

Hines, Walter D. "The Conflict Between State and Federal Regulation of Railroads." *Annals of the American Academy of Political and Social Science.* LXIII (1916), 191-198.

Irish, John P. "California and the Railroad." *Overland Monthly,* XXV (1895), 675-681.

Lesley, Lewis B. "The Entrance of the Santa Fe Railroad into California." *Pacific Historical Review,* VIII (1939), 89-96.

————. "A Southern Transcontinental Railroad Into California: Texas and Pacific Versus Southern Pacific, 1865-1885." *Pacific Historical Review,* V (1936), 52-60.

Lively, Robert. "The American System: A Review Article." *Business History Review,* XXIX (1955), 81-96.

McKee, Irving. "Notable Memorials to Mussel Slough." *Pacific Historical Review,* XVII (1948), 19-27.

Malone, Dumas, ed. "Joseph McKenna." *Dictionary of American Biography,* VI, 88. New York, 1933.

Moffet, S. E. "The Railroad Commission of California, A Study in Irresponsible Government." *Annals of the American Academy of Political and Social Science,* VI (1895), 469-477.

Netz, J. "The Great Los Angeles Real Estate Boom of 1887." *Historical Society of Southern California, Annual Publications,* X (1915), 54-68.

Norwell, James R. "The Railroad Commission of Texas: Its Origin and History." *Southwestern Historical Quarterly,* LXVIII (1965), 465-480.

Prendergast, F. E. "Transcontinental Railways." *Harper's Magazine,* LXVII (1883), 936-944.

"The Railroad Out of Politics." *The Wave,* VI (March 21, 1891), 10.

Ripley, E. P. "The Railroads and the People." *Atlantic Monthly,* CVII (1911), 12-23.

Russel, Robert R. "The Pacific Railway Issue in Politics Prior to the Civil War." *Mississippi Valley Historical Review,* XII (1925), 187-201.

Russell, Charles Edward. "The Railroad Machine As It Works Now." *Hampton's Magazine,* XXV (1910), 364-376.

————. "The Remedy of the Law." *Hampton's Magazine,* XXV (1910), 217-230.

————. "Scientific Corruption of Politics." *Hampton's Magazine,* XXIV (1910), 843-858.

Russell, James F. "The Railroads in the 'Conspiracy Theory' of the Fourteenth Amendment." *Mississippi Valley Historical Review,* XLI (1955), 601-622.

Smalley, H. S. "Railway Rate Control in its Legal Aspects." *American Economic Association Publication,* VII (1906), 327-473.

Wheat, Carl I. "A Sketch of the Life of Theodore D. Judah." *California Historical Society Quarterly,* IV (1925), 219-271.

White, Chester L. "Surmounting the Sierras, The Campaign for a Wagon Road." *California Historical Society Quarterly,* VII (1928) 3-19.

GENERAL WORKS

Boorstin, Daniel. *The Americans, The National Experience.* New York, 1965.

Bryce, James. *The American Commonwealth.* 2 vols. New York, 1907.

Gabriel, Ralph Henry. *The Course of American Democratic Thought.* New York, 1956.

Norris, Frank. *The Octopus.* New York, 1901.

Twain, Mark and Charles Dudley Warner. *The Gilded Age, A Tale of Today.* Vol. I. New York, 1873.

Index

*This symbol after a page number indicates a photograph of the subject mentioned.

254

Ward McAfee

Ward McAfee, a native son of the Golden State, fell under the spell of California's railroad story during his early years. From childhood he had heard stories of a time when "The Octopus" dominated the California scene. He began to investigate the accuracy of this folk belief while attending Stanford University and the culmination of his years of research is *California's Railroad Era 1850-1911*.

A professional historian by training, McAfee received his undergraduate and graduate degrees from Stanford University and is currently Dean of Social Sciences and Professor of History at California State College, San Bernardino. He has published several scholarly articles on the subject of railroad history which have appeared in the *Pacific Historical Review*.

The author is a railroad enthusiast of a different generation. While he is appreciative of steaming locomotives and the marvels of railroad engineering, his prime interest is the social, economic, and political impact of railroad development upon California. In his spare time, McAfee paints and draws for pleasure — even trains. One example of his artwork may be found opposite the title page of this book.